Threads of Time

Edited By J.P Harris

Copyright © 2021 by John P Harris

All rights reserved. No part of this publication may be reproduced, distributed, or transmitted in any form or by any means, including photocopying, recording, or other electronic or mechanical methods, without the prior written permission of the publisher, except in the case of brief quotations embodied in critical reviews and certain other non-commercial uses permitted by copyright law.

Disclaimer

Although the editor and publisher have made every effort to ensure that, the information in this book was correct at press time, as some of the content was provided by interviews who claimed to experience events. Some names and identifying details of people described in this book have been altered to protect their privacy and any other incidents that may be similar to the contents of this book are purely unintentional and coincidental.

ACKNOWLEDGEMENTS

I would like to thank the following and
really appreciate your help in compiling the book

Jon Austin (Daily Express), Jenny Randles, Betty Frien, Tom Slemen,
Jim Penniston (USAF/Retired), Deedee Doughty,
Kevin Montana www.messagetoeagle.com
Carl Grove, Mark Macey, Theo Chalmers, Dmitry Sudakov (Pravda),
Jerry Decker, Ellie Crystal (Crystalinks), Paul Gater, Stuart Kirkpatrick
on www.coolinterestingstuff.com
C.R. Berry, Scott Corrales, Andrew Collins, Dean Morgan.
Also to Gary, B Anna, H, Elizabeth, W, for the WW2 accounts.

INTRODUCTION	1
BRIEF OUTLINE OF THEORIES	5
BOLD STREET, LIVERPOOL	10
THE BRIGHTON VORTEX	16
TIME SLIPS RELATING TO WW II	19
TRANSMISSIONS	38
SID HURWICH THE MAN WHO COULD FREEZE TIME	45
THE BATH TIME MACHINE	50
THE VATICAN TIME MACHINE	58
DIMENSIONAL SLIPS	64
THE PHILADELPHIA EXPERIMENT	81
DIE GLOCKE; HITLER'S TIME MACHINE	90
THE IRAQ STARGATE:	98
THE STRANGE CASE OF RUDOLPH FENTZ	103
PORTALS	107
ARE THERE ANY OTHER THEORIES BEHIND TIME SLIPS?	123
THE ROUGHAM MYSTERY	139
TIME-HOPPING: THE AMAZING STORY OF KEN WEBSTER	150
THE RENDLESHAM FOREST INCIDENT	162
THE WOOLPIT CASE, SUFFOLK, ENGLAND	170
BIBLIOGRAPHY	175
RECOMMENDED READING AND LINKS	186

INTRODUCTION

This book contains examples of documented cases of possible time slips and experiences of interdimensional portals. Items from my compilations are from people I used to contact on phenomena based chatrooms and forums back in 1998-2001. I also conducted archive research in libraries accessing newspaper articles and websites.

I would cross-reference sources by comparing several versions of the incidents. For example, in the late 1970's a man pops out for a newspaper, and while taking a short cut near his flat in Chelsea, finds himself on the Kings Road, but 150 years into the future.

In the mid-1970's; a radio amateur called Ed, was startled when he received radio transmissions from a WW2 German U boat in the North Sea. I have discovered while recording content for the book that war zones and strong electrical activity seem to have a connection with time anomalies.

I have an impartial view on whether these events might be factual or the individual may have encountered some form of paranormal experience beyond the third dimensional haunting.

However a tangible explanation could be decades away. The main thing is I hope you find the cases interesting.

Sir Isaac Newton's conclusion is that absolute space, in its own nature, without regard to anything peripheral, always remains similar and fixed, which has been the standard perspective on time being linear, and has been unvaried for centuries.

However, the collection over the last hundred years of theoretical studies and research with quantum theory may modify this perspective. Time Travel has been in the human psyche for centuries in folklore tales and science fiction. In Hindu mythology, the epic Mahabharata, written and compiled in the 3rd century BCE. One of the segments tells of King [Raivata] Kakudmi who travels to heaven to meet Brahma.

Kakudmi returns to earth, believing that he has only been in Brahma's realm for a brief amount of time.

When Kakudmi returns, he finds everything has changed and discovers he has travelled 27 catur-yugas into the future, which is the equivalent of 324000 years in European chronology. Braham told Kakudumi that time exists on different planes of heaven and earth. In Jewish folklore, one story that dates to the 1st century BCE, tells of Honi ha Magel who fell asleep under a newly planted carob tree. He slept for 70 years and found the tree had grown; and was partially buried under an edifice of stones. He went into the village and found everything had changed, he was unable to find anyone who knew him, the local people thought he had passed away and built a tomb of rocks.

In 8th century Japan, according to a local legend, a fisherman called Urashima Taro. While fishing, falls overboard hitting his head on the side of the boat and is knocked unconscious. As he sinks into a deep chasm, Taro is rescued by underwater beings, who take him to a city at the bottom of the sea; he stays there for what felt like a day.

He returns to the surface and eventually goes back to his village and finds that everything has changed beyond recognition.

He discovers he has travelled 300 years into the future.

A book written by Irish born writer Samuel Madden in 1733 titled *'Memoirs of the Twentieth Century,* is centred on the imaginary world events of 1997-98. Described as a satirical novel, the main premise features the memos sent by the British representative while on assignment in the cities of Constantinople, Rome, Paris, and Moscow. The book has been categorised as one of the earliest works to feature time travel. An angel from 1998 visits the protagonist in 1728 and provides him with a series of documents. Later, the protagonist eventually passes on the articles to the Lord High Treasurer and other representatives.

INTRODUCTION

Written as a series of articles and correspondence, the structure of this particular book is described as epistolary, this format uses the method of diary entries and letters.

Madden, being an Anglican clergyman, depicted the world in the 20th century as governed by Jesuits, focusing on the dangers of Catholicism. He published the book anonymously; later Madden destroyed all of the copies just as the book was completed. In 1819 American writer Washington Irvine, who at the time was living in Edgbaston a district of Birmingham, UK. While staying there he wrote Rip Van Winkle that tells of a man living in the Catskill Mountains who one day meets two mysterious Dutchmen who offer and ply Van Winkle with drink. He wakes up 20 years later and misses the War of Independence, still believing that his town is still under British rule.

Looking Backwards was written in 1888 by Edward Bellamy using a theme set in the distant future. The protagonist Julian West is induced into a deep sleep through hypnosis. He wakes up in Boston in the year 2000. The book portrays society in the year 2000 as being utopian.

The main elements include technological references to a device called "electroscopic videoconferencing", which is interesting considering radio wireless technology was not commonly available until the 1920's, even credit cards were mentioned in various sections of the book.

It appears that Bellamy used ethereal means of time teleportation for his protagonist, while writers such as H.G Wells, and Edward Page Mitchell were using mechanical devices as a method of time travel.

Early Time Machines:

In 1881, Edward Page Mitchell wrote a short story in the New York Sun newspaper titled: *The Clock That Went Backwards.* It featured two boys who while visiting their aunt Gertrude, found she had a clock that dated to the 16th Century. The boys discovered that, when you moved the hands anti clockwise, you were able to reverse the flow of time. Later into the story, the boys travel back to 1574 and find themselves in the middle of the *Siege of Leiden,* in which they support the Dutch people against the Spanish.

Later in 1895, H.G Wells, this story illustrates the use of a mechanical device for time travel, by going forward or backward in time. The main protagonist in the original story is known unassumingly as the 'Time Traveller'. While entertaining guests

at a dinner party, he shows them a machine he developed that may have the ability to traverse the 4th dimension. The main fuel source is a mysterious green crystal called platternite, which is supposed to have radioactive properties. Wells also infers political analogies through the subtext between two main class structures, the Eloi and Morlocks. Perhaps, the technological aspect may also run parallel with the mechanical and scientific developments of that era, as the 19th century is synonymous with the Industrial Revolution.

BRIEF OUTLINE OF THEORIES

Black Holes Are Natural Time Machines [*1] According to Stephen Hawking, "Black holes are indeed, natural time machines." A black hole is a star much like our sun that has died and imploded into itself creating a massive and powerful vacuum that swallows up anything that crosses its path. Scientists believe that the powerful implosion of a dead star actually creates a puncture in the fabric of space and time. In a "Mail Online" interview, Stephen Hawking describes a black hole located in the middle of the Milky Way, situated about 26,000 light years from our Earth. As an example, a black hole is extremely large, about the size of four suns that have been crushed into one single point by its powerful gravity; nothing can escape a black hole, not even light.

Slowing of Time

This particular black hole mentioned in the article demonstrated a potential consequence on time distortion, by slowing down more than all other objects within its range. Still, no object can come close enough to the black hole to test the actual effects it might have. The gravitational pull will draw anything that comes close to it like a vacuum, and will completely crush the object. In order for a human-operated machine to use this black hole to travel through time, there would have to be a way to keep a spacecraft on the outer ring where it would not succumb to the crushing gravity and intense pressure of the black hole.

The current scientific viewpoint is that if a spacecraft was sent into orbit around the outer ring of this massive black hole, time for those inside the craft would slow down to approximately half the speed of time on Earth. This would make it impossible for the crew of any such experiment to return to the same Earth in which they departed. Everything on the planet would have doubled in age to that of the crew.

Frank Tipler's Time Machine

Frank Tipler is a Mathematical Physicist and Cosmologist at Tulane University, who discovered a mathematical equation previously undiscovered within the "Theory of Relativity." Tipler's calculations have revealed that time travel exists within the theory of relativity, in which "time-like curves," are present. His discovery has led to the theory of a time travel machine that would operate based on an object rotating around an infinite cylinder.

The Principle

Although the "Tipler Cylinder," is hypothetical and based only on theory, metaphysical scientists, whose approach is to study what is beyond material reality, believe that it would only allow for time travel at the length of the cylinder. For the cylinder to be productive and lead to more lengthy areas of time travel. The cylinder would have to be an infinite size along with use of negative energy, which is currently out of reach of becoming an actuality.

Mr. Tipler's study of possible time travel involves the theory that any object rotating around a "Tipler Cylinder," of infinite length, would allow for travel backwards in time. [*1]

Practicality

The Tipler time machine is impractical due to the infinite size involving the construction of such a cylinder. Still, scientists are consistently making new discoveries that could eventually reveal an equation that would alter the necessary size of the cylinder making it much smaller, and far more feasible. This type of discovery would allow for possible construction of a Tipler time machine. [*1]

Time Travel and the Large Hadron Collider

The overview regarding CERN over the past several years, has been subjected to speculation about the creation of a Large Hadron Collider which has been constructed between the borders of Switzerland and France, with the four major connectors being located in France. Most of us only learned of "Project Alice," or, "A Large Ion Collider Experiment," a few years ago. Since that time, there have been several speculations about the particle accelerator; including concerns voiced by Stephen Hawking, in regards to the possible discovery of a "God Particle," Hawkins stated, "Higgs Boson has the potential to destroy the entire universe."

This, of course, created quite a stir both within, and outside of the scientific communities. To date, the Large Hadron Collider tests are still on-going. However, there have been "strange happenings," that have been documented, in addition generating the idea that the Large Hadron Collider is not just about particle experiments, but may lead to discovering parallel universes, and who knows at a later phase discover the elements of time travel. [*1] examples of LHC experiments are revealed in other occurrences.

Scientific Experiments in Time Travel

The following items include a brief overview of previous and current experiments, as most of the stages of the research are within the areas of particle and quantum physics. In Australia 2015, Physicists at the University of Queensland in Brisbane led by Martin Ringbauer, have used photons to emulate time travel by using standard optical equipment on a lab bench by generating a pair of single photons, using a laser beam that passes through a nonlinear crystal. The idea is that the "younger" particle remains in normal space–time, while the "older" one disappears down a simulated wormhole. [*2] Parallel Universe Experiment Physicist, Dr Leah Broussard, who is based at the Oak Ridge National Laboratory in eastern Tennessee, along with a team of researchers who at the time of the report in 2019, were in the process of attempting to find whether or not a parallel universe exists.

The project is cited in science journals, and was referred to as the 'mirrorverse' experiment. The research objective was to find and solve the missing dark matter by attempting to open a portal. The method involved was to fire a beam of subatomic particles enclosed within a magnetic field, eventually passing through a 50ft tunnel.

As the particles hit the neutron detector, which is positioned on the opposite side of the laboratory wall. If the devices are calibrated correctly, some of the particles that pass through the wall may transform into a "mirror" version of the actual location, demonstrating the existence of a parallel dimension. [*3]

BRIEF OUTLINE OF THEORIES

Time Travel Can Be Invented

Professor Ronald Mallett a theoretical physicist based at the faculty of the University of Connecticut. While studying the intricate details of theories by Einstein and by using sets of equations, he believed it could be possible to construct a device that can go into the past. Prof Mallet was fascinated by the concept of time travel, this urge was enforced by a tragic event when his father, a heavy smoker, died of a heart attack at the age of 33. Ron, being overcome with grief; sought solace in reading books especially about science, one book in particular was HG Wells "The Time Machine." His aim was to build his version of a time machine and to reunite himself with his father and warn him not to smoke. After serving in the U.S Airforce during the Vietnam War, Ronald enrolled at Penn State University. In 1973 and at the age of 28 was awarded a PhD in physics.

He focused on the elements of Einstein's theory of relativity, especially the fundamental attribute of how gravity could slow down time. One of the core aspects of Professor Mallets' research was to use light rather than mass. One experiment was to observe a time traveling neutron in a circulating light beam produced with a ring laser. Prof Mallett created a desktop device, composed by arranging a series of mirrors at certain angles, and by directing a light beam that could warp within the surrounding space.

While observing subatomic particles, it was discovered the particles tend to have a short life span. Moreover, if these elements exist longer than expected when positioned within the circulating light and have continued beyond the expected time span, it could be that they have flowed through a time loop into the future [*4]

BOLD STREET, LIVERPOOL

The following accounts have been provided by the courtesy of Tom Slemen. This busy street in Liverpool has been a subject of bizarre timeslip cases involving varied timelines and experienced by a range of individuals. Case #1

In July 1996 an off duty, police officer called Frank was out shopping in the city centre along with his wife Carol. As they approached Bold Street, Frank decided to visit the HMV shop for CD's while Carol went into Dillons Bookshop. Sometime later Frank decided to meet up with Carol, and walked alongside the Lyceum building, which leads onto Bold Street. As he continued to walk towards the meeting place, he had a feeling that something was peculiar, and noticed how silent it was. Suddenly, a small box van appeared from out of nowhere, and sped along his path missing him by a few inches. The make of the van was the type of vehicle from the 1950's, which also had the company name 'Caplans' on the side panel. As he walked into what should have been Bold Street, he noticed the passers-by were dressed in clothes that were considered old fashioned.

Men wore trilby hats, gabardine macs, while women's fashion included chiffon headscarves, hats, and full-length skirts. The clothes and hairstyles appeared to belong to the early to mid-1950s. By this time, Frank was beginning to feel slightly detached and disorientated, he continued to cross the road and made his way towards the book shop , but noticed what should have been the shop sign for Dillons Bookstore, appeared to have a sign for a haberdashery store called Cripps, which ceased trading in the early 1970's. While Frank looked through the window, he noticed there were no books, just handbags and shoes. While glancing to the side he noticed a young woman wearing modern clothes, she was also staring at the shop sign in equal disbelief. She looked at Frank, smiled at him, and said, 'I thought they sold books here, 'So did I,' he replied, realising he was not alone.

Moments later as he looked through the window from inside the shop onto the street, it appeared that everything went back to normal, everyone outside was wearing modern clothes. Frank being a police officer deals with facts, and a non-believer in the paranormal, but his experience gave him another perspective.

In 2006, a 19-year-old shoplifter and drug user by the name of Sean was targeting the stores around the city centre. He was loitering in one store on Hanover Street attempting to do a "lift." A security guard, who was tracking Sean's movements, noticed that he stole something and tried to stop him at the entrance. Sean dashed out towards Bold Street, and rushed across the busy road heading towards Brooks Alley, which is a dead end. Now out of breath, Sean recalled his first experience of having a tightening sensation in his chest, and described the atmosphere as dense and heavy. The security guard was still running after him, Sean ducked down behind the nearest wall and waited a couple of minutes. He looked again, and noticed the guard had disappeared so Sean sauntered off in the direction of Hanover Street feeling pleased that he had given the guard the slip.

However, as he crossed the road to Bold Street something did not feel right, looking below he noticed the pavements and roads looked old, each car that passed him was either a Morris Minor or a Hillman Imp. He noticed how people seemed to be wearing peculiar looking clothes. It was raining heavily, and it seemed as if it had been raining all day. In addition, the road works known as the Big Dig was not there.

As he crossed the road towards Bold Street, another strange feature was the traffic lights, not only did they look old fashioned, he could not remember these lights being on the precise location, as they were removed years ago.

While these strange things were going on, Sean began to panic, and continued to look around to find anything he could recognise.

He took out his mobile phone, but there was no signal. Spotting a newspaper kiosk on Ranelagh Street, he went over and looked at the front page of the Daily Post. The date was Thursday 18th May 1967.

He suffered another panic attack realising he had gone back 39 years and wanted to return to his normal place back to his friends, as they were his only family being that his parents had disowned him. He ran towards Brooks Alley in an attempt to reverse the situation, by going back to the point from which he arrived, then continued running towards the Adelphi hotel and stopped close to H. Samuel, the Jewellers. He tried his phone once again, this time it worked, and was relieved that he was back in 2006.

Oddly enough, Sean looked down the other end of Ranelagh Street; he could still see people dressed in the styles of 1967. Sean, not intending to unravel the paradox, headed towards Brownlow Hill, and decided to catch the bus. Later Sean approached the Liverpool Echo giving an account of what happened.

The security guard who chased Sean confirmed that 'As I tried to pursue the lad, down Brooks Alley, he just disappeared into thin air'. One of the journalists at the Liverpool Echo later confirmed the descriptions outlined by Sean as accurate; the landmarks and shops described by Sean were there in 1967. [*5]

Liverpool Time Slip: Mothercare, Lord Street

One afternoon, Imogen, a 17 year old from Garston was shopping for some baby clothes for her sister Abigail who had just had a baby. Imogen was pleasantly surprised to see that a new branch of Mothercare had opened on the corner of Lord Street and Whitechapel, and eagerly walked into the store. She chose a few, and several other items, all of which were incredibly low-priced. Imogen presumed that the items and accessories were sold at introductory bargain prices because the store had only just opened – until she tried to pay with her credit card.

The girl behind the counter looked at the card with a distrustful expression, and immediately went over to her manager and showed her the card. The manager inspected the credit card, she shook her head, and handed it back to Imogen, 'We don't take those love'.

Imogen only had a small amount of cash on her; she put the items back and left the store. When she returned home in Garston later that day, she told her mum Debbie about the incident at Mothercare and how even though her card was valid it was not accepted. Debbie replied, 'there was no Mothercare on the corner of Lord Street?' 'There used to be, but it moved years ago'.

'Well, it's back again,' said Imogen, and her mother disagreed, because she had an account at the HSBC Bank – which stands exactly where the old Mothercare store once stood. Imogen and her mum disagreed that much, they went to town together the next day – and sure enough, there was a bank where the Mothercare store had been 24 hours ago.

Only then did Imogen realise she must have experienced a timeslip, which could explain why the staff had rejected the credit card and why the prices were so low as Imogen had probably gone back to the early 1980's.

Possible Theories: One possible factor, quartz can be found in most building materials. If under pressure and subjected to varying environmental conditions can produce a minor electric charge, moreover if activated, quartz elements resonate at altered frequencies, which may affect certain people. To use a comparable example, in the late 1970's and early 1980's, a large number of UFO sightings were reported within Todmorden, a former mill town located in the county of West Yorkshire, UK. Moreover, sightings were also reported in the surrounding areas of Bacup, Littleborough, and Rochdale. In a television series "Strange but True" that was broadcasted in the mid-1990s. One of the researchers, who participated in the programme, was accredited for having a scientific background.

The researcher highlighted the connection with the local geology that consists of Millstone Grit, which is defined as being a course grade sandstone and has a high composition of quartz pebbles and mica inclusions. The hills around the mid-Pennine region, especially around Todmorden have outcrops and boulders distributed along the peaks and at surface level. In the documentary the researcher revealed, 'that the sightings may be due to electrical activity possibly generated from the quartz elements which could create balls of light'.

Most of the structures in the area were built with this stone. If for example, a rock outcrop or building foundation is located on a geological fault line, and if a shift occurs within a fault line, this has been known to produce electromagnetic energy when the quartz elements are disturbed. The electric fields generated by the electromagnetic emissions of quartz are very intense. In one laboratory test, the result from the emission signals of the electromagnetic radiation spectrum readings were within the 100 kHz to 1 MHz frequency range.

This activity could percolate into the local environment and create manifestations or strange sightings. Moreover, certain weather conditions may cause the quartz inclusions on structures above ground, to generate a residual resonance field and if the field is prominent pending on environmental conditions, could affect the human mind.

To include additional factors on the Liverpool timeslip cases may relate to the underground railway network around Central Station [Ranelagh Street], which seems to be in the pinnacle of the time slip incidents. One researcher highlighted that the outline of the track system appears to run in a circular formation in the centre of Liverpool. The central point of voltage influence is situated approximately around Bold St. Due to the high voltages transmitted along the tracks, perhaps the by-product of electromagnetism from the "live rails" in the locality could produce some sort of magnetic or what is known as a torsion field. Moreover, the possible combination of geological factors [quartz inclusions] and electromagnetism may generate some form of frequency, which might create a vortex, distorting perceptions, or even resurrecting fragments from past events.

THE BRIGHTON VORTEX

An article that was published on the 2nd of May 2013 by Anna Roberts in the Brighton and Hove Argus highlighted a complaint that was submitted on the local council forum FixMyStreet.com. The grievance was posted anonymously and considered, rather peculiar.

The report claimed that a large hole suddenly appeared on Montreal Road, situated in the fashionable Hanover district.

The unknown correspondent emphasised that he had witnessed what he described as a portal.

Fix My Street, deals with matters such as faulty streetlights, litter, fly tipping, potholes, and other environmental related issues. The full account as follows [*6] 'I was walking my dog around the Hanover area, as I approached Montreal Road I noticed a hollow space appear out of nowhere in the middle of the road'. 'Then suddenly, spinning threads of lights appeared from the hole '. 'It was like something out of the films, when you could end up in another place or something like that.' 'I was wary of getting any closer to whatever it was, just in case my small dog [Affenpinscher, a toy breed of dog] would have been sucked into it'. At first I thought it was an artist's installation for the Brighton Festival, but I think this 'portal' is a real hazard'. He concluded the post with 'I look forward to your reply/response.'

' On the following Thursday [9th May], Mr Anonymous posted an update claiming that on his second visit to Montreal Road, again while walking his dog, he was shocked by what he saw. One side of the house was covered by a strange yellow light, followed by a serpent type creature coming out of a wall on the side of a mid-terraced house. [*7]

I am concerned that if a snake appears from a wall, what else can come out of this portal?' 'I need some suggestions for the next course of action.'

Predictably, this left the council leaders mystified as not many hoax articles appear on their website and the standard comments from the other forum users included the usual "drugs and booze" induced hallucinations.

The council decided not to follow up the enquiry then added 'residents can still use the usual contact methods of telephone or direct email via the official council website.'

Ben, who is a Brighton resident, explores theories and other probable facets that are linked to this case. It was the aspect on how the feature was presented, as Ben remarked 'What I find interesting, there is no mocking overtone'. Anna Roberts is a crime reporter for The Argus, who wrote the article. This invites the question, why a quirky approach? Moreover, written by a reporter who usually covers themes of a serious nature or did Anna take the day off from serious news?

Curiously enough, two local residents published an article on another website years before the Fix My Street incident occurred. The two young women, who encountered the vortex, suspected that it could have been a secret portal used by the local Masons for decades. [*7]

Possibly, during a ritual, one of the members did not follow the exact procedure for shutting down the portal, hence leaving the vortex open. In varied conditions, the anomaly could have been reactivated, and one particular night two young women Deedee and Lindy saw a strange swirling light rising from the road. Deedee entered the vortex, while using her long woollen scarf as a safety line to prevent from being drawn into the portal. Deedee ventured near the opening and spotted a necklace in the centre of the 'vortex'. She reached out, grabbed the chain, and managed to get out in time before the portal vanished.

As Deedee and Lindy examined the necklace, they noticed a masonic emblem on the pendant. What they may have found would have belonged to the leader of ceremonies, possibly lost from the last portal opening ritual.

Another interesting connection, Montreal Road is located close to a tower structure, known locally known as the "Pepperpot." Designed and built in 1830 by architect Charles Barry in the grounds of a villa constructed for the owner of Queen's Park fabricated by using Ranger's Lime Concrete [*8].

The function of this sixty foot structure holds a range of theories, a list of uses include; a water tower for the mansion house that was located close by, or a ventilation shaft for the network of large Victorian sewers beneath Brighton. Before the tower was built, a large house stood in the exact location, date uncertain of the original building, but the old house was demolished in the 1800s, nevertheless the tower stands on its foundations.

It was also rumoured that the residents of the previous house were part of an arcane occult group who used to conduct rituals there. Which rendered theories about the tower having some sort of occult connection e.g. was it some sort of conduit or amplifier? Moreover, it has been renowned that Brighton had a reputation for strange cults, similar to the 'Hellfire Club' that were active in the late 18th century. Perhaps some of the previous or on-going strange rituals may have activated the first phase of creating 'The Brighton Stargate'.

TIME SLIPS RELATING TO WW II

The following cases are given by people who had felt they might have either experienced a shift into a segment of a battlefield in Europe or an air raid shelter in London, even years after the war.

East End Bombsite: Napoleonic Timeslip

While on an 'anomalies' themed chatroom back in 1998.

One of my contacts called Elizabeth would discuss cases on a regular basis. While conversing about strange incidents that happened in and around London, Elizabeth just happened to mention an occurrence that her aunt Beryl [actual name concealed to hide identity] had experienced while growing up just after the Second World War. Elizabeth sent me a full account of her aunt's experience, highlighting she may have slipped back to the early 1800's while exploring a bomb site with her elder sister Daisy.

Elizabeth also added 'as I got older I used to ask aunty Beryl about what she saw. Beryl would reply with a simple

'I don't think I was seeing things, it felt real'. Sometime later Elizabeth asked her aunt for the full account and took notes on every detail. 'It was 1947, and though the war had ended, it was still a tough time. As a seven-year old, Beryl had returned to her parents' home after being evacuated from Mile End Road , situated in London's east end. During the Blitz, Beryl was sent to live with relatives in Lincolnshire. On her return, she felt strange. It took some time to settle back in. Like all other children, she played in the semi-derelict streets; Beryl recalled that her friends would use one of the battered Victorian lamp posts by lashing some old rope on the struts to make a swing. Beryl always wanted to tag along with her older sister Daisy and explore the bombsites, as for most kids they were an adventure playground. 'Sometimes you can find hidden treasure' said one of Daisy's friends and added '

Someone I know found a load of silver 'thrupneys' in an old vase'. Beryl, used to keep 'mithering' her elder sister to tag along, Daisy always said no and kept repeating 'it's too dangerous.'
However, on this occasion Daisy said 'Come on then but don't wander off because you will fall down a massive hole.'

Beryl described this particular day. 'It was cold, we walked what seemed for ages down the grimy damp streets as most of the buildings were in various stages of falling down,' 'The houses that escaped being hit were propped up with massive wooden frames.' In addition, you would get 'half a house' with the top room window frames with shards of glass sticking out like icicles, tethered to ripped curtains. They ended up on a block of houses near Wellclose Square located in Stepney. 'It was an odd place' said Beryl.

She remembered how strange it was that some of the buildings were not touched even after extensive bombing, but remained empty as most of the buildings were boarded up. Beryl noticed one tallish looking house that had a gap in the wall like a 'giant mouse hole.' Beryl found this particular house entrancing. Daisy was close by, but decided to explore an old outhouse and told Beryl to stay put. Beryl then decided to clamber across the garden of the tall house, ignoring Daisy's 'orders', she began to sneak into the hole that was under the window. Some distance away, Daisy and her friends were throwing rocks onto the roof of a shed; Beryl peeked into the gap, as she was small enough to slide through. While crawling through the gap trying to avoid the loose bricks and cobwebs, she managed to squeeze halfway into a room. Suddenly, Beryl noticed a woman wearing a white linen cap, and a baggy blue dress, peering over a big metal pot that was positioned above a large open fireplace.

TIME SLIPS RELATING TO WW II

Taking a second glance, two other people appeared out of nowhere, one woman who was wearing a grey flannel dress, and a crumpled bonnet. Moments later, a man appeared in a green coat with ribbings on the front, and a shako hat walked into the room. Beryl described the scene 'It was just like out of the Gainsborough films we used to watch at the pictures.'

[Gainsborough Studios, a London based film Production Company who on occasions would produce historical dramas].

Beryl added, 'Inside the furniture looked really old-fashioned spindly chairs, striped wall coverings. Even though a fire was roaring away in the huge fireplace, I did not feel any heat.'

As she sneaked in for a closer look, suddenly a small boy, dressed in a blue calico gown gave Beryl as she later described 'an inquisitive look' then began waving at her, and started shouting. Somehow, if the toddler was making a noise, the other two people did not hear him and did not take any notice. The boy continued to point and shout, though Beryl could not hear any sound, but crept back slowly and ran off. 'Hey Daisy 'as she scrambled across the foot strangling weeds and other debris, 'there are people in that empty house.' Beryl tugged Daisy's jumper and pulled her towards the garden. 'What people?' 'It's an empty house?' said Daisy, 'she was a bit miffed' Beryl recalled. Daisy still reluctant to follow Beryl across the weed strewn garden 'you first Daisy,' said Beryl. Daisy said 'Alright then I am not scared' and climbed through the 'mouse hole'. Moments later, Daisy replied 'there's nothing here just a dusty room full of bricks and rubble'. Beryl then went inside, all she saw was a pile of wood, rubble and bits of coal strewn against the wall , it also smelt damp, which ruled out there ever been a fire. They went back to the same place two days later.

The gap in the wall was not there, Beryl added 'it looked intact as if there never had been any hole or any form of damage,' 'I even took a closer look at the exact spot, 'nothing, it seemed untouched.' I asked Elizabeth what she thought. Her viewpoint was that the location of Wellclose Square had a curious history and highlighted the connection of the "people" Beryl had seen. Elizabeth studied the description of the man by researching historical records as Beryl, may have been looking at a soldier who might have been off to war, or was he on leave? In either case, he was dressed in the British army uniform that would have been dated to the Napoleonic war - (1803-15).

TIME SLIPS RELATING TO WW II

NETHERLANDS CASE 1970

The following case was sent in by a contact via a paranormal based chatroom. The screenshots of the discussion were on a Windows 95 computer, which unfortunately I lost all of the files due to a malfunction; however, I managed to retain a transcript in a notebook.

Anna (not wanting to submit her full identity) was from the Netherlands, and always insisted what she experienced was real. Anna also maintained with humour 'Yes everywhere in Europe has this notion that Holland, appears to be connected with the lenient view regarding cannabis, 'I do not even drink, let alone drugs' so that rules out being stoned.'

Anna grew up on the outskirts of Rotterdam, Netherlands and at the time of her encounter, she was 19 years old. One Thursday morning in June 1970, it was around 8:00 am in the morning. While on her way to work, she always cycled along the N207, a highway located close to the Maas River. It was a bright and clear day, however within a few minutes, what appeared to be a circular patch of mist drifted across and hovered in the middle of the road.

'I did not take much notice, and cycled straight through it'. 'I also saw how the cattle in the nearby field were beginning to make such a noise as if they were in danger.' 'However, give or take about ten minutes, I began to feel strange, out of place, detached.' Anna never sensed this before having been on this route countless times, she also felt a sudden wave of feeling scared and miserable. 'At this time, the road was unusually empty and silent. Suddenly, this gaunt looking man appeared, dragging a cart, the type of cart meant for a horse to pull, let alone a frail looking man.'

'It was stacked with oddments, and old fashioned furniture, battered and tatty.' 'Two women also appeared, they followed the cart, looking bedraggled and weary, huddled in heavy coats and wearing hats that reminded me of an old photograph from about the mid-1930's'. 'The type of clothes my aunty would wear.' As she cycled past, one of the women gave her a strange look.

Anna did not want to ask anything, but wondered 'Are these people vacating from a flood?' 'Then within a couple of minutes, I heard a rumbling sound, two grey coloured, what appeared to be German tanks from WWII just materialised out of nowhere'.

One of the emblems on the side panel looked like a "Y" the markings were partially battered and scratched; the tanks appeared to escort the refugees'. 'My immediate thought 'are they making a war film?' However, the curious thing about the tanks, they did not have the presence of being solid objects; they appeared to 'judder' like the faulty reception on a TV set. On the turret or hatch, one of the tank crew stood up and scanned the area around him. Anna described his appearance of having an ashen grey complexion almost deathly looking ,' his face was embroidered in total shock when he saw me' ; Anna also recalled feeling a sense of dread and cold.

She panicked; as the soldier looked in her direction, and felt a myriad of mild electric shocks across her head.

I asked 'how long did these shocks last?' Anna replied' not sure it felt like 10 minutes.' 'However, at this point, I was really terrified and tried to speed off in the opposite direction, towards my village which would have been about 2 kilometres'. 'I must have only gone about 1 kilometre'. 'Even though I was dazed, curiosity made me go back to the actual spot.' 'Moments later, I cycled back to the location; I looked around for clues such as clods of earth, scratches on the road surface'. 'Then I estimated the direction or route the refugees were going, they should be even passing me at this point.'

TIME SLIPS RELATING TO WW II

She also noticed that the mist and feeling of dread had gone. Anna glanced at her watch; it was now 9:50 am. Later on when she arrived at work apologising for her absence, 'I had an accident and fell off my cycle.' The manager gave Anna the day off; as he noticed, she looked dazed, and insisted that she should go to hospital.

Keeping the experience a secret, Anna decided to make some enquiries around town by having casual conversations in the local store especially chatting to people who would have been old enough to have experienced the Nazi occupation. In her free time, she would conduct research in the library.

She happened to meet an old school friend who later relocated to South Africa and was an amateur photographer and filmmaker, and one of his main areas of interest was producing documentaries. Anna asked him 'were there any films being made recently? 'He replied, 'not as I know of, if there were, I would be the first to know.' Then on reflection, Anna said 'I wish I had my camera with me.'

LONDON UNDERGROUND

I have been in various tube stations across London and have sensed what I would identify as a powerful atmosphere, especially in Whitechapel tube station. I also recall some odd sense of perception when I visited Waterloo tube station that also had a strange ambiance. These visits triggered the insight, what if anybody else may have had strange experiences in the London Underground? I could imagine a list of strange cases that go beyond the odd ghost sighting.

I found this interesting case of a possible time slip at Waterloo underground station experienced by a young woman from Surrey. While travelling up to London on the train to meet her boyfriend at Waterloo Station, the plan was to meet up and catch a connecting tube train to somewhere in the west end of London. As the couple met each other, they rushed to catch the next tube train. Unable to recall on which side of the station they were on, she described the descent on the escalator as slow and protracted. As the couple were near the platform, the woman noticed scraps of paper drifting around slowly, and then shifting in the opposite direction. This prompted the first hint of weirdness; anything that moved was in slow motion. It was at this point she felt something was not right; a shift in the atmosphere, the feeling of dread and gloom seemed to be everywhere. As they waited on the platform, the strange feeling became amplified 'It was too quiet, even when there were groups of people moving around, they all seemed unresponsive. It was almost like being underwater.'[*9] At the foot of the escalators, were lines and lines of string. Bits of cloth and rags draped over them, the corridors, and any other spaces that were available were set up as makeshift shelters.

It was not just isolated areas; it appeared that the whole station was a refugee camp. Still unaware, which platform they were supposed to be on, the woman described how it seemed to be taking longer than normal to walk to their connection. This moment had a tense, strange feeling and added how the place had flipped into something more unfamiliar.

Moreover, she was in two minds on whether to tell her boyfriend about her unusual perception. [*10] "Standing in a corner was a man in an official uniform – I don't really remember him just that he was bald, and had shiny buttons on his jacket, whose presence made me feel no less uneasy. I was trying to convince myself that if he was there, it would mean that all the weirdness of the clothes- lines were somehow explicable. "Only afterwards, when my boyfriend and I compared notes did we realise that we both sensed something old-fashioned about his outfit and demeanour."

"As the couple boarded the train, she began to feel an increase in panic that was amplified while watching a man who sat opposite them. His face was red and close to tears, the boyfriend looked directly at the man giving him a nod of sympathy. The woman now realised that her boyfriend was also experiencing the strange events, but he kept discreet, and whispered," Look at him, too."

While another man further down the carriage had an expression as if he was in fear of his life. It still did not occur to both of them what was going on. 'We just both thought that maybe we had a fleeting premonition or something, but felt we should get off the train - immediately.' Only afterwards, as they collected their thoughts, we realised then, the feeling of complete strangeness from the moment we headed down into the underground station." [*11] One thing that occurred to the young woman was that they might have slipped back in time possibly to World War 2. During this time, most of the underground stations were used as air raid shelters.

BROADCAST FROM SINKING U-BOAT
LOCATION: NORTH SEA

One case that I documented back in 1998 originated from a contact on the AOL Phenomena chatroom from a man who at the time was based in Aberdeen called Gary who sent me an email, which summarised an account about his uncle who was a radio amateur.

In 1975, a welder called Ed who lived not far from Newcastle upon Tyne, UK, was a keen shortwave radio enthusiast who was studying for the amateur radio operator's licence.

Once completed this would allow him to transmit signals on other allocated bands and frequencies. Part of his exam would require Ed to be proficient at sending and receiving Morse code.

After work, usually, about 7:30 pm, he would go to his shed at the bottom of the garden, switch on the radio equipment, and wait a few minutes until the valves warmed up, then tune in; this was the downside when using old-fashioned valve sets.

He picked up the shortwave radio in a junk shop. I asked Gary 'what type of radio was it?' He replied, 'A big cumbersome, ex-army surplus thing, probably from WW2.'

Ed was unable to send live transmissions on air even though the radio had the ability to transmit, if he did use the transmitter he would be in serious trouble with the Home Office. In the meantime, he would scan different frequencies and listen to a range of coded messages. While tuning, he would pause on a station that transmitted Morse signals, and then decode and interpret the transmissions into letters and numbers. Most of these messages would be gobbledegook to an ordinary person; however, Ed could identify the country and location of the broadcasts.

Towards the end of the week, he would stay up into the early hours of the morning, dragging in all sorts of transmissions at varied frequencies. It was in mid-April 1975 at 1:15 am, while tuning in to 29.5 megacycles, a sharp burst of blips and dashes came through the speaker extension.

TIME SLIPS RELATING TO WW II

The signal was so loud- the paper cone vibrated. Strangely enough, from 6.30 pm in the evening, there were intermittent episodes of sheet lightning that seemed to continue later on into early hours.

Ed went outside to check the earth cable was secure, thinking 'What if the sheet develops into a bolt lightning?', but there was no sign of heavy rain. Moments later, a series of Morse signals came through, they may be local transmissions, or perhaps someone was using a signal booster that may be located hundreds of miles away. He wrote down and decoded the transmission. When he deciphered the code, it read "VVVV EE 631 1130 TT CA" ...taking into account a possible 30-second pause. Then another stream came through 20 seconds later "TNOC GNIT NIAM." Mystified by the codes and their sequence, Ed began to flick through a reference book by cross checking if any similar broadcasts were listed. Gary recalled that Ed panicked thinking that he may have discovered a top-secret message, he also pondered 'Was it from NATO'or Eastern Bloc?' It was at 2:30 am when another transmission came through; Ed recognised the pattern of the message and began to translate the code.

The third message on interpretation had a slight variation, which came through as "VVVV EE 601 1025 — TTCA TNOC GNIT" in this stream, part of the code details had transformed. As the message ended, everything went silent. He moved the dial to 28.9 megacycles; the radio was still silent, not even any background noise like wobbling oscillations or distant "monkey chatter" then began to wonder if any of the components had burned out? He tested the radio on another channel, switching over to an ordinary radio station on the AM band that worked fine, and then changed back to the short wave frequency. [*Megacycle is a unit of frequency, equal to one million cycles per second; Megahertz is now preferred in technical use*]

I asked Gary 'Did your uncle Ed manage to record evidence?' 'He did, he set up a reel-to-reel tape recorder to snag any more transmissions, he placed a microphone close to the speaker, and kept the recorder button on standby'. Gary then highlighted; 'Within five minutes, a crackling voice message came through, it seemed to have an echo 'It's gone…yes affirmative 'over'…

Ed told us how strange it was, while looking at the dial it was set at 30 megacycles'. Ed tuned the dial back to 29.8 m/c hoping there may be a repeat transmission. It was now 2:50 am; he rewound the tape recorder, found the short burst message, and marked the segment with a felt-tip pen. He replayed the transmission and thought, 'Should I contact the authorities?' Nevertheless, he decided at this point not to bother.

A couple of weeks later and still urged on by curiosity, he decided to write a letter to a radio ham magazine about the strange broadcast. He sent a brief article about decoding Morse transmissions 'Does anyone know what these are? "VVVV EE 601 1025 – TTCA TNOC GNIT". Two months or so later, Ed received a letter from a man called Arthur who said. 'I might know what these codes are, as identified in your message'.

They decided to arrange a meeting in a pub on the outskirts of Hull, a port town further down on the east coast of the UK, which is a fair distance from Ed's location. They met two days later; Arthur said he was a radio operator in the Navy during WWII. Ed had converted the original recording from the cumbersome reel to reel onto a cassette tape; he also brought along a portable cassette player.

I asked Gary 'could you outline the meeting? '

Gary replied, 'Ed described the meeting as peculiar. 'We sat in the corner of the pub. I played the message on the cassette, then I handed the notes summarising the decoded message: "VVVV EE 631 1130 TT CA and TNOC GNIT NIAM",

I also outlined that a series of messages arrived about 10-15 minutes later "VVVV EE 6011025 – TTCA TNOC GNIT" 'Just curious to know where they come from?' Arthur paused, and then exclaimed, 'These appear to be transmission codes... from a German U-boat!'.'

'How on earth did these come through? 'Ed played the recording again; 'it's gone...yes affirmative 'over.' Play that again,' said Arthur, who appeared to be shocked. Ed continued to play the snippet ten times. 'How did you get that? a message like that would have been scrambled?' That is me!-If this is real, I was 100 miles from the Tyne estuary...

'I can't tell you anymore!' Arthur looked shocked, then rushed his drink, got up and thanked Ed for meeting him, then made a hasty exit. This left Ed perplexed, later he tried to contact Arthur several times, no reply Ed attempted to trace him with no luck. What invites the question, did either of them consider that someone might have been broadcasting an old recording? I asked Gary what made his uncle consider at that time the transmission was genuine. 'He did have doubts at first as he is a no-nonsense type of guy,' Gary also added

'It was the way Arthur reacted, and his expression made Ed think,' is it possible that it could be genuine?', and the main question that alternated with Ed, 'what if it did happen...who knows?'

THEY EXPERIENCED AN AIR RAID FROM THE FUTURE
BY CYNTHIA MCKANZIE

Journalist J Bernard Hutton along with his colleague, press photographer Joachim Brandt was on an assignment in Hamburg in 1932. Hutton was writing an in-depth feature on the Altona shipyard. They spent most of the afternoon interviewing executives, and workers building a wide-ranging profile for their story. [*12]

Later on when they had finished, both of the journalists drove across the expansive site. As they were driving along the main route towards the exit gate, Brandt heard a loud whirring sound of a siren, he commented to Hutton 'I wonder why the siren is activated?' 'Is it an emergency drill'?

At that time, there were no war plans. What happened next took them by surprise. Suddenly a deep droning sound went across the sky, out of impulse; Brandt looked up and saw a swarm of planes coming in from the distance. As the bombers flew closer, Brandt was surprised when he noticed the RAF emblem on the wings. Curiously enough, they did not see any defensive installations as they were touring around the docks. After what seemed like only seconds, huge explosions erupted all around them as bombs spilled out all over the dockyard. One of the big warehouses was the first to be hit, then another building close by blew up, both asked the obvious 'why are they bombing the shipyard-what's going on?'

Hutton began driving at speed, weaving across the road as more bombs fell; dust and smoke blustered across in all directions making it tricky in controlling the car. Hutton kept a look out for the nearest place of refuge.

Now they were a sitting target, while a huge fire ripped across the docks and nearby areas. As the two men managed to find a safe location, Brandt took a rapid series of photos of the incredible event. As they drove towards what was part of the main gate they spotted a security guard all he did was shout in German, 'Get out-find shelter now!' Both of the men looked behind and noticed the massive fuel storage unit was engulfed in flames.

Moving further out towards Hamburg, the sky remained dark with ribbons of smoke spreading across the skyline.

As they arrived into the city centre, everything was quiet, no craters or bomb damage in fact it was as if nothing ever happened. Brandt turned and looked towards the shipyard and noticed there were no signs of damage, no ruined buildings, no buckled dockyard cranes, and no clouds of black smoke.

Later that day Brandt shot two reels of film, including the shots of the bombing raid. Brandt's photos showed nothing, the editor wanted to confirm Brandt's and Hutton's account of the incident by contacting the shipyard. The outcome was that there was no raid or any sight of RAF planes in the vicinity.

The rest of the newspapermen found Brandt and Hutton's story somewhat amusing, putting their experience because of knocking back too much Schnapps at the local bar. Later the two men were promptly dismissed as a cause of potential embarrassment.

Later in 1943, Hutton, now based in London, was examining the story on the recent RAF raid in Hamburg and the Altona shipyard. His reaction was déjà vu and shock as the photograph in paper was exactly the same scene of destruction and the same place he and Brandt experienced 11 years earlier.

Recommended website www.messagetoeagle.com

THE SECRET GARDEN: LEEDS, WEST YORKSHIRE, UK

[*13]During the Second World War, Leeds was Britain's third largest city, and the target of Nazi Germany's Luftwaffe, the biggest air raid was in 1941. A total of 25 tons of bombs fell on the city, the count included: 100 houses were destroyed, 4,600 sustained damage, and around 65 people were killed. In November 1945, the Camp Hill area of Leeds saw many rows of old terraced houses being demolished. Stripped of their doors, floorboards, and window-frames some provided dubious areas of adventure for local schoolchildren, a group of whom were busily exploring the vicinity.

One day, a young boy was jumping from joist to joist on the upper floors and staring down through the window gaps at the masses of smashed bricks and timber below. [*14] The boy was called Peter Turner, who was puzzled while he looked down on what seemed to be a small, well-cultivated rose-garden in full bloom. Despite the wintry season, an old man was lovingly tending the garden. Despite a subsequent search among the mounds of rubble — even below the very window-gap he had originally looked through— Peter was unable to find any sign of the beautiful garden, which of course, none of his friends had seen. We are all psychic to a greater or lesser extent, and he may have experienced some sort of time-slip to a bygone era, when there could have been a beautiful rose-garden there in place of the small backyard more usual of a terraced property.

Alternatively, the garden could even have existed in an earlier era before the terrace of houses itself was constructed. Sometimes there can be several layers of haunting in the same place with ghosts materialising from different time frames. The man tending the plants, was wearing what would be considered, as old-fashioned clothes, and on reflection while reading history books, he noticed that the gardener's clothes were possibly from the late 18th century or early 1800's.

Figure 1 Merrion Place 1850: Reproduced with the permission of the National Library of Scotland

Years later in 1964, the actual site underwent demolition and eventually a shopping centre was part of the redevelopment plan. Peter went over one day to watch the building work, while reflecting over the fact on what he saw was a time-slip. The house, which Peter explored at the time, is now part of the Merrion Shopping Centre in Leeds city centre. Moreover, according to the map dated 1850 he may have seen the gardens of Belgrave House, which is within close proximity to Merrion Place (Fig1). According to records, the house may have been built around 1720, though uncertain regarding the original name; however, in 1847 it was listed on other maps as Belgrave House.

TELEPHONE CALL

This was sent in to Tom Slemen as part of the collection of Merseyside Timeslips. A Radio City listener named Emma Black sent Tom Slemen a cutting from a 1970s magazine concerning a timeslip, which apparently allowed a telephone conversation to take place between two people spaced thirty years apart. The following summary of this strange story may seem like an episode of The Twilight Zone, but I have heard of three other similar cases. An old woman named Alma Bristow of Bidston, Birkenhead, tried to phone her sister (who had recently lost her husband) in Frodsham, Cheshire. Alma always had difficulty-dialling numbers on the old British Telecom analogue telephone because she had stabbing arthritis in her fingers. Alma had mistakenly misdialled her sister's number, as a man's voice answered. The man said "Captain Hamilton here!". Alma asked if her sister was there, but 'Captain' Hamilton replied haughtily, "This is not a civilian number. Who are you? 'Alma gave her name, while at the same time she could hear the sound of an air raid siren 'to take cover'.' Alma joked, 'Sounds like World War Two there'. There was a pause, and then Captain Hamilton replied, 'What are you talking about? 'The air-raid siren sounds like the war's still on' replied Alma. She was about to hang up...until Hamilton continued. 'Of course the war's still on, where did you get my number from?' 'The war ended years ago, in 1945.' Said Alma, suspecting she was a victim of the Candid Camera Show.

TIME SLIPS RELATING TO WW II

Captain Hamilton whispered to an associate, and then resumed the surreal conversation. 'It isn't 1945 yet'. 'If we trace you, you will be thrown into prison for this lark, do you know? You're wasting valuable time, woman.' 'Eh? It's 1974.

The war's been over for years." Alma retorted, and then she heard the unmistakable rumble of bombing coming over the phone. 'We'll deal with you later, don't worry." said Captain Hamilton, and he slammed the phone down. Alma listened eagerly for him to pick up the handset of his telephone, but Hamilton never did. Alma never knew if she had been the victim of an elaborate hoax, or whether she had really had talked with someone in wartime Britain. [*15]

TRANSMISSIONS

The following cases relate to radio and TV transmissions that appear to circumvent time and space. They could be classified as either precognition or pre-emptive telepathy. Moreover, to invite the question, is there a link with radio waves and electromagnetic activity that might create some form of time distortion?

FLIXBOROUGH: TELEVISION TIMESLIP INTO THE FUTURE:

On Saturday, June 1st 1974 at 4:50PM, a tragic event took place in the village of Flixborough north Lincolnshire. A large explosion destroyed the Flixborough Works of Nypro (UK) Ltd. The origin of the explosion was initiated by a fault in the reactor unit. It was later discovered after a site investigation that the cause of the explosion originated from a rushed modification on one of the fittings that resulted in a leak, which dispersed a cloud of flammable hydrocarbon vapour across the site. As the cloud of vapour lingered across the complex, within minutes one of the furnaces ignited the flammable vapour, resulting in a massive explosion with the equivalent of 15 tonnes of TNT. Twenty-eight people were killed and 36 injured, the toll would have been higher if the disaster occurred during the normal working week. Meanwhile, Mrs. Lesley Brennan who lived in the nearby town of Cleethorpes was busy sorting things out for the weekend.

With the TV on in the background, she was suddenly stopped in her tracks by a newsflash, which displayed film footage of an explosion of what appeared to be a large industrial complex. This was at 10:30 am, other parts of the news item presented buckled towers and flames shooting up into the air. The news footage appeared to be fragmented or as Mrs Brennan described it as 'flickery'. Later, about 1:00 pm, she asked her neighbours if they heard anything about a massive explosion, with a predictable bemused expression, the neighbours replied with 'No?'

Mrs. Brennan, without realising, had just witnessed the Flixborough explosion-six hours before the tragedy occurred, and was shocked when the news bulletin came on at 4:50 PM that day.

By coincidence on the same day about 203 miles away, Reg Presley, lead singer of the 60's band The Troggs also experienced the same precognitive incident. The bands were known for the hit singles 'Wild Thing'- 1966 and later in 1967, 'Love is all Around'. Wet Wet Wet covered "Love is all Around" in 1994, the pinnacle song for the film; 'Four Weddings and a Funeral'. It was a huge international success and spent 15 weeks top the British charts.

Reg Presley was recovering from injuries, due to an incident that happened at a gig the previous week. A gang of Hells Angels gate-crashed their performance, creating havoc. The aftermath of this horrible incident, resulted in two of the band members being stabbed, Richard Moore, the guitarist, nearly died; another was bottled and Presley emerged with a broken nose and three cracked ribs.

Reg was relaxing that Saturday lunchtime, dozing off in front of the TV, later about 1:00 pm, a news bulletin suddenly appeared, displaying a caption: *'An explosion at Flixborough, North Lincolnshire, 28 people have died and 32 were injured'* this was four hours prior to the incident. Later that day, Reg switched on the TV for the ITN 6:00 PM news. Reports relayed the disaster as happening 8 minutes ago.

The news story highlighted the actual time of the explosion as 4:52 PM. Out of surprise, he said to his wife 'How did I see the report about a disaster four hours before it happened?'

Reg Presley always had an interest in the unexplained and held a theory regarding the time distortion he experienced. His notion, what if for example, something relating to gravitational time dilation as gravity can bend spacetime, and therefore time itself? This may have altered the broadcast signals.

On the other hand, most physicists would reject the idea of radio waves traversing time. However, there have been similar cases of TV and radio transmissions arriving hours before their schedule, could this be related to quantum entanglement?

For example, could the radio waves be part of some sort of causal loop? [*Causal loop: is when a future occurrence is the source of a past event, which in succession is the cause of the future event. Both events exist in spacetime, but their origin cannot be verified.*]

Quantum entanglement is when subatomic particles are connected in a variety of conditions that may affect each other, even when separated by great distances. It has been speculated that multidimensional quantum teleportation is theoretically possible. In a common frame of perception, this would go against classical physics; even Einstein described quantum entanglement as a "Spooky Action." Recently, faculties of research in quantum physics have conducted experiments on a microscopic scale, by 'teleporting' one photon to another location; the Vienna Institute conducted the experiment within the faculty for Quantum Optics and Quantum Information, which is part of the Austrian Academy of Sciences, in a joint venture with the University of Science and Technology of China.

In 1974, the author Andrew Thomas published a book titled 'Beyond the Time Barrier'. In one section of the book, he outlined the possibility that electronic manifestations and even images from future events can appear days or hours within the present timeline.

For example the Flixborough incident, the comparative distance of the two locations Cleethorpes and Andover having no direct connection , the two and half hour difference between Mrs Brennan and Reg Presley's experience, why at varied time intervals.

Could it be possible, the people who experienced the event prior to the tragic accident may have precognitive abilities that manifested into actual footage rather than just a 'feeling' of something was about to happen?

TRANSMISSIONS

SHORT WAVE RADIO INCIDENT

A radio ham experienced time distortion while experimenting with ultra-high radio frequencies; this incident was highlighted on the website *keely.net*. The website outlines technical information to people active in a range of electronic experiments and alternative technology. The forum users provide examples and the results of their projects.

In November 1997, a radio amateur called Bob was experimenting using a variety of electronic components. While conducting research he noticed and took interest in a device called the Bajak Time Travel Flux Capacitor, invented by John Bajak who claims the device can distort time by using a basic electronic circuit. Later on, Bob continued to build a full wave/full frequency radio, as this was part of an ongoing project.

Finally, he created a device that was so powerful it could receive and transmit on frequencies even up to the electromagnetic light spectrum, which in terms of radio is extremely high. Prior to going live, he carried out final checks on the main components called magnetrons. Magnetrons were used in older versions of radar equipment, the component can be found in old-fashioned TV sets and in microwave ovens. Their function in a microwave oven is to generate extremely high frequency radio waves; they are the main device for the heating process by generating a wavelength of 5.8 GHz (Gigahertz). By altering the layout and adjusting the wiring, he acknowledged that by using the magnetrons could be manipulated to enhance the radio to access the higher wavelength region.

Reflecting on an article he once read on Nikola Tesla, Bob thought about emulating one of Tesla's experiments. The research carried out by Tesla was included in a book titled: "Wall of Light" which also contained elements of metaphysics. In 1895, Tesla believed that he had created a device so powerful that the electromagnetic field could alter space-time.

While Tesla experimented with magnetic fields, he believed that the space-time barrier could be 'altered' and accessed by creating what he referred to as a 'Trojan Horse' which eventually could open up a gateway to a different timeline.

Later, Bob constructed the device, consisting of a large box with two equally large coils at either side, (imagine a similar layout to bookends).It was now early morning, around 2:15 am, the weather at the time was raining with bursts of forked lightning. Around 3:00 am, Bob attached a speaker to the device and began tuning into various frequencies expecting the usual short wave stations.

At 3:15 AM, a sudden loud crackling burst through the speakers, so loud it rattled the small ornaments in the room. Out of panic and in desperation Bob severed the cables in fear of disturbing the other residents. He carried out checks on all the circuits, and went outside in the pouring rain to check if the aerial had been hit by lightning, he also thought he had seen a 'glow' around the aerial.

According to readings on his meter, the aerial was in the stage of 'induction'; it appeared that the storms had affected it.

Electromagnetic induction is the production of an *electromotive force* (EMF) across a conductor when it is exposed to a varying magnetic field (the storm), the conductor in this case was the aerial that was subjected to a change in the magnetic field. The weather conditions would have produced ionization in the local atmosphere. As ionisation usually occurs in thunderstorm conditions, the electric field becomes very strong and when the conditions are ready for the air to begin breaking down. The electric field causes the air to become separated into positive ions and electrons, hence the air becomes "ionised."

The combination of the external conditions had increased the voltage of the circuit up to 44 Volts DC when in fact the radio was only supposed to have an input of 18 Volts DC.

TRANSMISSIONS

Later at around 4:00 am, while testing the device using a multimeter, Bob noticed additional bursts of static discharge. The rain had stopped ages ago but the odd burst of thunder continued.

As he moved further back from the device, Bob noticed and was in awe of what happened next. A peculiar glow began to hover above and across the coils-

the glow began to form into an orb that was approximately 10 centimetres in diameter. This continued for about seven seconds then disappeared. The orb appeared to have three to four shades of light, separated by a pulsating gap that had the form of being transparent then shifted into semi-opaque producing additional circular bands.

Bob could not identify the properties of the object however; he compared two factors that could eliminate the possibilities of it being either;

#1, St Elmo's fire: This has a purple colour (usually confused with ball lightning) this would not materialise as a perfect orb shape.

#2. Electrical ionization of nitrogen, Bob dismissed this as a nitrogen event, if affected by ionization and if it were nitrogen, the orb would not glow blue or produce circular fields. The next bizarre thing emerged when all the clocks moved from 4:15 am to 10:00 pm, it appeared that time had moved backwards six hours. Out of curiosity, Bob tuned in to one of the local radio stations; he was stunned on what happened next. The station was playing the 10:00 pm news bulletin as if it was live. Bob was now baffled, he immediately looked at the other two clocks in the room. They also displayed the time as 10:00pm, he even felt the atmosphere at the present time was different, just like your perception of certain times of the day and night. He tested the device again and noticed an increase in the voltage, which read 44 Volts DC. Around 5:00am he heard the radio anchor announce the time as *"Two-Forty Five A.M....here at our station K.N.O.P Port Angeles Washington State"*.

Bob then decided to dismantle the aerial, after that he fell asleep.

The following day, one of the neighbours pulled him to one side and asked him if he noticed anything strange as the other resident's T.V sets were malfunctioning and projecting strange images usually lasting from six to twenty seconds around 10:00pm? (The previous night).

Casually, Bob declared that he did not use his transmitter and could not do so, due to the bad weather conditions. Finally, could it be on certain occasions the Universe oscillates electromagnetically on certain primary, and harmonic, frequencies?

As suggested not only in three dimensions but also in the additional context of TIME. For example, like Bob, constructed a device so powerful that may have the ability to shield himself from the oscillations on a local time scale, hence the possibility of experiencing different time zones.

Thank you for Jerry Decker who sadly passed away on the 19.06.2017, for permission of the original article

SID HURWICH THE MAN WHO COULD FREEZE TIME

'The ability to change the past and get an insight into the future has often resulted in the creation of the most remarkable time-altering machines.

A very strange case involving time travel and power to change timelines was reported later in 1977 the case caused a sensation worldwide.' Has Sid Hurwich the creator of the time-altering machine really found a way to alter historical events?' In 1969 at the Besh Tzedec Synagogue in Toronto a 64-year-old appliance repairman and retired company director Sid Hurwich stands proud on the bema (platform) while receiving an award from the Protectors of the state of Israel on behalf of the Zionist Organization of Canada. Sid Hurwich's contribution was a device he invented that he donated to the Israeli military.

Details of the mechanism were kept secret up until a few months later when the Toronto Star noticed the story about the clandestine raid on Entebbe by Israeli commandos and further research revealed a connection to the Sid Hurwich device and to the Israeli military. News agencies across the world also noticed the article and within 24 hours, the story went, in today's terms, "Viral." An in-depth account of the operation including the use of Sid's device appeared in the prestigious UK based magazine The Economist, listed under their regular news segment, Foreign Report. Components of the article had allegedly originated from a confidential diplomatic journal, as quoted: *"All could be learned was that Sid Hurwich's invention was used by the Israelis in the raid at Entebbe last year"* [1977] [*16]. Operation Entebbe or Operation Thunderbolt was a successful counter-terrorist hostage-rescue mission carried out by commandos of the Israel Defence Forces (IDF) at Entebbe Airport in Uganda on 4th July 1976.

A week earlier, on the 27 June, an Air France Airbus A300 jet airliner with 248 passengers had been hijacked by two members of the Popular Front for the Liberation of Palestine. [*17] The article also provided an outline on how the device transmits electronic rays to alter and dismorph the natural and surrounding magnetic fields and to distort the central gravity point of weapons, and to damage internal mechanisms.

An additional capability of the device while used in Operation Entebbe was the ability to disable tanks, ground-to-ground missiles and disrupt radar systems. Moreover, the beams of electromagnetic (EM) strands that were projected could be meshed together forming an invisible screen, creating a safety zone that could deflect bombs and missiles.

The Israelis kept the whole process under secrecy and refused to reveal any basic principles of the Hurwich Ray even to allies or internal staff at academic scientific research facilities. Sid's daughter Silvia Winkler Hurwich presented a biographical account of her father's early interest in technology.

It began when Sid was 9 years old, he used to collect and repair old bicycles and any old household appliances that people threw out.

By the end of the 1930's having no technical qualifications other than a standard high school diploma, Sid had the reputation as the main appliance technician in Toronto and even across Canada. During the outbreak of World War II, he was known as the man 'who could repair anything'.

Ontario Hydro took an interest in Sid's skills and informed the Canadian armed forces conscription board not to put Sid Hurwich into active service.

SID HURWICH THE MAN WHO COULD FREEZE TIME

The management at Ontario Hydro pulled a few strings to keep Sid with the company, later he was in charge of the public service department. Due to government rationing and restrictions on the use of metals, as all types of metal were used for the war effort. These restrictions meant that the productions of household goods were also limited, so it was a make do and mend situation. Sid's repair business expanded, and by 1947, he built up a company called Shock Electric, which grew into one of the largest companies in Toronto. He created another business that manufactured electrical components called SIDCO.

However, in 1950 at the age of 36, Sid Hurwich suffered a near fatal heart attack. His next decision was to sell off the businesses, and take early retirement.

In 1969, there were a growing number of bank robberies around the Toronto area. The criminal's key targets were the bank deposit boxes.

One evening in the same year, Sid Hurwich had an idea, which he quoted in an interview for a magazine. 'Something just clicked, 'I picked up the phone to the police, 'I knew a lot of the boys .... and I told them I think I can stop those thieveries in about half an hour.'

He immediately telephoned a friend in the police department who happened to be a high-ranking officer, and said 'I might have something which might be useful in stopping these robberies'.

Later, two police officers paid him a visit then asked 'How is it you could help us Sid?' A week later, he built a device, which cost him around $50 dollars. On completion, he contacted his friend from the police department to test his theory. Two police officers and a bank security official arrived at his house.

Sid then summoned them to his basement workshop and showed them an outline of his invention, hidden under the workbench and covered with a bedspread; Sid unveiled the invention and gave an outline of its capabilities.

Later in an article, Inspector Bill Dalton described, When Sid flicked a switch and said to me ... 'Take out your gun', then added, 'I took out my gun and noticed the trigger was jammed'. As I placed my revolver on the workbench- I then tried to lift the gun off the bench, I couldn't, it weighed a ton'. Hurwich then announced, 'Now look at your watches' somehow even time was altered.

The men arrived 25 minutes before their watches stopped, time must have stood still when they arrived at Sid's house. Sid commented 'this condition was beyond the mechanisms of the watches'. One of the rookie officers commented 'what's happened?' as they lost nearly half an hour, Sid then added 'You are now late by 25 minutes'. [*16]

When the men left Sid's house Mrs Hurwich overheard the men as they walked towards the front gate' I think the Army should consider looking into this'. Hurwich contemplated the idea of contacting the military about his device, and quoted

'It did occur to me that it could be used in warfare', and continued to upgrade his invention.

Sometime later, confident on the additional modifications he contacted his brother in Israel. One motivating factor was, if anything, the State of Israel needed the device the most. With the on-going conflict and being surrounded by belligerent Arab nations who were determined to push the Israeli nation into the sea. In a hotel room in Tel Aviv, and adjusting to his first time visit to the country, he prepared himself for the appointment with the Israeli military.

Later that day, two high-ranking Israeli army officers arrived at the hotel. Sid gave a demonstration of the apparatus, on conclusion; Sid gave a final outline of the additional capabilities of the device.

When the meeting had finished, the officers took the plans, design specification, and the actual working model with them. The invention was portable enough to be carried by hand.

Sid outlined 'It is not an invention as such, just a reworking of the basic principles of electricity and electromagnetism but restructured.' The primary unit of the device works by using a concentrated electromagnetic field, he also found while calibrating the mechanism, a means of projecting an EM (Electro Magnetic) field across a target situation.

As for example, in a document that recorded the debriefing of the Entebbe Raid, mentioned how Israeli planes flew into the target location without being detected. Dr Howard White, a consultant engineer based in Toronto, was sceptical but mystified. Dr Howard outlined one of the factors in the device, affirming that Sid Hurwich had used 'an extremely high and compacted electromagnetic field, but was unsure what could have generated it.'

Dr Howard also added that jamming a few guns and blocking long-range radar devices is a huge step forward.

It could be that Sid Hurwich may have independently discovered the Aspden Effect* named after British physicist Dr Harold Aspden while experimenting with electromagnetic motors. One key discovery was the swirling energy found inside an electromagnet. A similar outline would relate to the driving flow of an electromagnetic current, similar to a boat propeller creating a powerful vortex in water. This appears to be how Sid Hurwich created such a massive change in the flow of time within a local area. Dr Howard added, 'Then again anything is possible'. Curiously, Sid did not patent the device and did not believe in patents 'what could happen, someone else would make another copy or variation? He also did not bother with any financial gain; as he said 'Money is not use to me at my stage in life'.

Thank you to chief editor, Kevin Montana for permission for the article. http://www.messagetoeagle.com

THE BATH TIME MACHINE

Back in 2011 a satellite channel by the name of Controversial TV that was operated by an independent production company Edge Media Television and was relayed across the UK on Sky channel 200 and on FreeSat via Eutelsat 28A. Theo Chalmers hosted a discussion programme titled "On the Edge," which highlighted paranormal related subjects and to examine possible explanations on case studies. Theo interviews Terry Le Riche Walters, who has written books on his personal experiences, one of his key titles includes "Who on Earth am I." In one of the episodes of On the Edge series 15, Terry outlines his encounter 60 minutes into the discussion. He revealed how he became involved in a bizarre time travel experiment in a terraced house in Bath, Somerset, UK. The Reverend Lionel Fanthorpe: a writer and TV presenter (Fortean Times ITV, 1997) who happened to be with Terry Le Riche Walters at the same time also gave his version of the experiment 'On the Edge' (Series No 18 Part I). The narrative begins when Terry attends a UFO group and gives details about his book and related experiences. Later on, Theo asks Terry about a time machine. Terry unfolded the story while attending a book signing and a Q and A session with the group.

Later into the conversation, one of the attendees was a physicist who was deliberating on how solid matter could be altered by removing the molecules. He began to demonstrate this by taking a glass tumbler off the table and began to coat the inside of the glass using a gel-like substance; Terry could not clarify what was in the formula. Moments later, the physicists poured water into the glass, which was still clear and intact. Within a few moments, water began to seep out of what was described as a myriad of microscopic holes. The physicist then stated 'This is the advanced aspect of my research'.

THE BATH TIME MACHINE

After the demonstration, one of the other scientists said to Terry, 'would you like to see a time machine?' Terry replied 'Yeah' I would'.

A few days later, he received a phone call from the one of the men who arranged to set off later that night then added we will be travelling to a location in Bath.

As they were half way into the journey, the gearbox went, the car breaking down prompted one of Terry's travelling companions to say the mechanical failure was some sort of omen- 'It's not to be'. Terry, dismissed the breakdown as 'these things happen just call the AA', just postpone, and go another time. A week later Terry along with two other men, hoping this time there should be no problems, Terry also emphasised in the interview 'you had to be invited'.

As they arrived on what was described as an innocuous looking street on the outskirts of Bath. Terry described the property, 'I went in with a security guy and Lionel Fanthorpe'.

'It was a small, end terraced house', as you walked inside it seemed to be out of proportion'. Theo interjected and described the experience in comparison to the Tardis [The Tardis, a teleportation device used in the cult TV programme Dr Who]. As Terry walked down the hallway, the house owner advised him, 'just carry on walking to the other end of the room, or else you will be sick'.

Terry said he met a man called Gordon Pringelli, who at the time was in his 80's. Terry said that 'Sadly, Gordon is no longer with us'. Gordon Pringelli , told Terry how the "time machine" came about, Gordon said that he had a lucid dream, something like an out of body experience in which he floated to a location somewhere near the Orion constellation.

'Gordon believed that humans have a connection with Orion and that he actually went inside a UFO and met a group of extraterrestrials who gave him a blueprint for a device'.

Terry added, 'Gordon passed the blueprints to a couple of guys who worked for Hewlett Packard', who constructed and assembled the device. Allegedly, the founders of 'Hewlett-Packard' were interested in experimenting with time-travel'. Later, as Terry entered the main room, he noticed the seats were arranged in a circle.

Above the circle was a large glass dome on the ceiling and with the other additional fixtures created a strange perspective.

Terry added, 'I sneaked upstairs to see where the dome went', it should have gone through the roof as it was that deep' but it didn't'. In the centre of the room was a device in which Terry described as a 'healing machine' the actual blueprint that Gordon was given, was for a healing machine, however, it also had the additional capability of being used as a time-travel device. An audio tape activated the healing machine's crystal circuitry, playing what Terry described as old rock and roll music beats, Terry then emphasised the 'music of today is based on these beats' like the human heartbeat.

The device contained precious metals and jewels, and when activated, threads of light came down from the dome onto the subject who wanted to be cured, he also added, "when sound is fed into the device; it creates the helium lights to form patterns".

As Gordon Pringelli told Terry, the device could cure most ailments, as Terry's agent suffered from migraines for ages. The agent decided to try the device to see if it would work. Terry described what happened when his agent sat under the machine. The agent turned black and then returned to his normal colour, he told Terry that he hasn't had a migraine since. Terry gave another example about the healing machine, 'one guy put his arm through, and it vanished for a moment, a few seconds later his arm reappeared'.

Theo reviewed Terry's experience on how he walked into a Tardis-like room, and then prompted 'What happened next regarding the time machine?' Terry said he went into the same spot.

THE BATH TIME MACHINE

'There was me, Lionel and the security guy who sat in the space, the seats were positioned in a circular formation.

'We were seated directly under the dome. As the music was played through the lights,' a sort of calming music', even Andrew Lloyd Webber has been there, and was fascinated on how the lights were activated by the music'. Terry also mentions that a heart specialist visited the house; he had an ongoing experiment within the dome. He installed a recording of an actual human heartbeat in varied forms of condition to add to the lights.

Then by analysing the formations of the lights to the actual sounds.

'I sat there waiting for something to happen, thinking I am probably still here looking at nothing'.

Couple of minutes later, Terry claims he was in ancient Rome and added 'I have been here before, so I recognise the place'. 'I went in there at 12:00pm midday, thinking I was in there for an hour'. 'I realised when I looked at my watch it was now 6:00 pm, so where did that missing time go?' The others who attended the session also experienced the same trip to ancient Rome, but they did not meet or even see each other. Theo then prompts the question 'Was it physical experience or a manifestation?' also highlighting 'despite Rome being cosmopolitan even in the ancient times; you would stand out wearing Levis and a Ben Sherman shirt?' Terry concluded, 'we were there, I don't think anyone could see us.'

But one thing after that trip we were all exhausted and still felt like that for hours even when driving back home'.

In part 1, series 18, Lionel Fantorpe's interview outlines his version of the Bath time machine. It was 31 minutes into the programme when Theo mentioned to Lionel about his previous discussion with Terry le Riche Walters a few weeks earlier highlighting the time machine.

Theo asks Lionel, 'Terry named other people, including yourself and to confirm this, was you there? 'Lionel immediately replies, 'Indeed I was there.'

THE BATH TIME MACHINE

Lionel Fanthorpe's version:

Lionel begins by describing the device 'As a vast computerised set of kit', and illustrates how he met the inventor, who happened to be a retired jeweller, and was knowledgeable about computing'.

'Being a former watchmaker, he had the ability of repairing highly delicate and complex movements of expensive watches'.

Lionel reflected on the key motivation of the inventor, 'Not only having been absorbed from his former profession as a watchmaker, moreover

'whether the man's interest in his work gave him the motivation in pursuing the study and the philosophy of time, as this may have led to the notion of building a time machine'. Theo asked, 'Did you travel back in time?' Lionel replied, 'I didn't' but I believe Terry did experience some form of time travel. 'I believe a group of men who were friends of the inventor, claimed that they experienced some form of time travel'. Lionel added, ' What the inventor managed to do was not create a device like HG Wells time machine-which you and I could step into, and move back and forth a thousand years'.

Lionel added, 'If astral travel exists, and if a certain individual is highly perceptive, and feel they can move outside their body'. 'A concrete explanation would be, ' if you remembered some place you visited in the past and enjoyed being there, especially having a vivid memory of a certain place'. Lionel used this concept, 'When I was a small boy I used to visit the music hall with my father'.

Lionel described the atmosphere being there, the noise and the powerful sights of the acts. Taking it a stage further Lionel speculated that the device amplified the ability or enhanced the perception of a person to 'astral project" to a certain time'.

Theo added, 'While off air, Terry mentioned another experiment, when someone who used the time machine was sent back to an unknown location, and was physically attacked. In fact the person who went there was badly beaten and that would not be in your head or in a dream?'

Lionel's response was 'If there was another development of the machine that could move the physical body, it was one I did not see'. Theo asked Lionel regarding the structure of the house, and why it altered the perception of anyone who entered the place. Lionel gave a brief example, when he used to give lectures in psychology in which one lecture focused on having certain levels of mental states that can alter your perception and outlined an example of a museum in Cardiff called TechniQuest.

One of the rooms in TechniQuest, you experience while walking in one direction you seem to 'grow' and if walking in the other direction the room becomes enormous. Lionel then adds 'It's that all of the perspectives are all "wrong." 'Perhaps the inventor altered his laboratory and rooms in Bath possibly to emphasise the Tardis effect'. 'So it was while visiting TechniQuest I had a glimmering notion on how the inventor had created it'.

THE BATH TIME MACHINE

Editor notes: I recall a documentary film titled; *Alien Time Machine: Encounters from Another Dimension*. It was broadcasted a few times on Controversial TV around 2013. The film revealed the actual device within the dome and a single wooden chair, which was used for conducting time travel experiments. One of the interesting aspects of the film is when a participant in one of the trials describes going back to a street what might have been during the mediaeval times. I am uncertain of the location. However, after the experiment the man is interviewed. He looked dishevelled, giving a full description on how he was 'attacked by a mob on a muddy street'. This may have been the person as mentioned in the interview with Lionel Fanthorpe, when somebody went to a location and ended up covered in bruises. This could be the advanced version of the device that may have had the ability to travel back in time at a physical stage. The house in Bath no longer exists and was demolished some time ago.

An overview, the Bath Time Machine reminds me of the similar technology used on the 'Chronovisor' that was developed by two priests and a team of scientists after WW2. The device was also known as *The Vatican's Time Machine*. Content provided with kind permission from Theo Chalmers further links www.vervepr.co.uk

THE VATICAN TIME MACHINE

It is rumoured that somewhere in the Vatican there is a "time-seer" device, which enables its users to access past events and actually view scenes from history. There are numerous articles featured on websites, magazines and books hinting that the Central Intelligence Agency (CIA) apart from having the capability of accessing mobile phones, smart TV's and other devices on citizens and organisations across the world may have a hand in other projects. According to the author Alfred Lambremont Webre, the CIA has access to a device, which can traverse space and time. [*18] Alfred Webre has written a number of books on time travel; he is also a Law Graduate from Yale University and a member of the District of Columbia Bar. As Webre carried out research, he later discovered that in the late 1960s the CIA was in close contact with the Vatican. In addition, he also found out that the Vatican provided the US Intelligence agency with a device that used a process called "quantum access," which can enable humans to go back and forward in time. However, not in the material sense, but using a "time-seer" or in today's terminology a virtual device which is supposed to access traces left behind by past events and view scenes from history.. It has been implied that the Central Intelligence Agency (CIA) "was founded by the Vatican." Webre then adds, 'What the Vatican did is they subcontracted the technology and gave it to the US Pentagon and CIA'. [*19]. The Vatican being the gatekeepers of this advanced and arcane technology wanted to convey their knowledge of the chronovisor to the countries they considered allies, which include the U.S and British intelligence agencies.

As Weber indicated that, ever since the Secret Treaty of Verona, [1822] most of the European crowns all have links to the Vatican and would continue to retain their reverence. This has been ongoing for centuries, and includes countries that are categorised as republics. MI5 and MI6 and the CIA are really creatures of the Vatican secret service [*19] and one of the objectives would be to assist the Anglo-American Empire, and to keep control over the time bending technology to the loyal states.

What is the Chronovisor?

Father Pellegrino Ernetti and Father François Brune created the device just after the Second World War. The project also had assistance from twelve of the world's most leading scientists, two of them included Enrico Fermi and Wernher von Braun.

Fermi, an Italian physicist, later moved to the U.S and assisted in the development of the first nuclear reactor. According to conspiracy website discussion boards, mention that Fermi was also a member of the Freemasons. Wernher von Braun, the German aerospace engineer who developed Nazi Germany's long-range missiles the V1 and V2 then later in the post war years, worked for the U.S government. Wernher von Braun was also the key player, working with NASA [National Aeronautics and Space Administration] on the early space projects. A disclosed report: described the chronovisor of being a cabinet with a screen, however; another version defines that a circular CRT (Cathode Ray Tube) was placed on the top of a column structure to establish a revered aesthetic.

A cabinet containing the controls would have been positioned within close proximity of the device. The controls included a series of levers and buttons, when calibrated the operator tuned into a specific timeline and location. When the target was located, the internal "aerial" was able to receive and decode the electromagnetic radiation, and sound waves. These being the layers of chronological residue embedded within a specific location.

It may have used a similar principle of the tape recorder, by gathering trace elements of historical recordings that were projected onto mineral-based material, especially brick and stone. Moreover, paranormal researchers highlight a relative premise, wherever you have had activity with moments of intense emotional incidents, these events will leave a residue.

This in some cases can be recorded on audio equipment; perhaps the device may use a related process with higher capabilities.

The operator would "tune in" to a particular point by using the sequential dials of time, dates, and location. Then, by gathering and receiving faint residue of the electromagnetic signals from buildings, roads and other structures within the target location, and according to the operators, the device could also focus and track specific people. As Father Ernetti conducted one of the first experiments, he claimed that he observed Christ's crucifixion and managed to capture a photograph. Father Ernetti submitted the photograph to La Domenica del Corriere, an Italian weekly news journal on May 2, 1972.

This so-called peek into the past was subjected to immediate criticism and inevitably challenged whether or not the claim contained any truth.

Moreover, on analysis, a researcher compared a mirror image of a woodcarving by Lorenzo Coullaut Valera, which was identical to Fr Ernetti's crucifixion photograph, this immediately casted doubt on Fr Ernetti's claim.

Using the chronovisor, Fr Ernetti "travelled" to 169 BC and witnessed a scene from a play "Thyestes", by Quintus Ennius. The play is described as a Roman tragedy with a Greek subject; Ennius was regarded as the father of Roman poetry. Dr. Katherine Eldred of Princeton University is the author of the English rendition of Thyestes. Eldred believes that Ernetti actually wrote the supposedly ancient play himself, and pointed out that the text appears to be a lot shorter, in comparison to Ennius scripts that were more detailed and longer.

Archaeoacoustics and the past interpretations
Controversy

One aspect regarding the chronovisor, part of the process may have used the principle of archaeoacoustics. Archaeoacoustics is the notion that ancient artifacts and structures may have audio traces embedded or encoded into the artifacts and local environment. For example, stone circles and other ancient sites, especially objects like pottery. Moreover, the idea that a pot or vase could be played back like a gramophone record or a phonograph cylinder, by any level of sound, that could be inertly transferred onto the clay while the pot or vase was being moulded or turned on a wheel, or in the process of drying. The pot may have absorbed sounds from the surrounding ambient frequencies. This notion was highlighted in the New Scientist magazine (1969) where David E. H. Jones examined its possibility in the light-hearted "Daedalus" column.

"A trowel, like any flat plate, must vibrate in response to sound: thus, drawn over the wet surface by the singing plasterer, it must emboss a gramophone-type recording of his song in the plaster. Once the surface is dry, it may be played back." — Jones, 1982 [*20]

This article by David E. H. Jones brought the attention of Richard G. Woodbridge III who claimed to have already been working on the idea and said that he had sent a paper on the subject to the journal Nature. The paper never appeared in Nature as it was considered too 'fringe' for publication.

However, the August 1969 edition of the journal Proceedings of the IEEE printed a letter from Woodbridge entitled "Acoustic Recordings from Antiquity." In this communication, he wanted to demonstrate the potential of what he described at the time as *acoustic archaeology*. Woodbridge conducted his experiments while making clay pots. In the second experiment, he observed the 60 Hz hum from the motor that drove the potter's wheel; he replayed this by using a wooden spatula connected to headphones and a stylus that was positioned onto one of the pots, and then placed over the pattern.

He claimed to have extracted the hum of the potter's wheel from the grooves of the vessel. Another set of experiments included the sampling of sounds from oil paintings. One method was to paint a canvas using a striated or painting in streaks technique, while playing music at a high volume. An audio snippet from a painting could be replayed using a conventional record player crystal stylus that was connected directly to a set of headphones. Woodbridge claimed he recorded the word "blue" while analysing of patch of blue colour in a painting
[Proceedings of the IEEE, Vol. 57(8), August 1969, pp.1465-6.] [*21]
Woodridge also outlined a similar experiment he performed in 1961 claiming a successful reproduction of an audio imprint by using a crystal phono pickup and a spatula that he termed a 'wooden 'needle'. In 1993 Gothenburg, Sweden: Professor Paul Astrom (Archaeology) and Professor Mendel Kleiner (Acoustics) conducted an experiment where they created a clay cylinder and transposed 400 HZ signal onto the soft clay by using a basic electrical stylus. By taking into account that even if the clay cylinder was fired, the audio traces may not be affected and still remain intact. Later by turning the cylinder on a mandrel, a signal of 400HZ, still could be heard and measured with a drop between 1-2 HZ. On review critics have outlined, if using low frequency ambient sound, especially in the process of wet clay, it will be susceptible to fading, leaving the imprint smeared beyond recognition, moreover
if a maximum force was used in the stages of creating an object on paper, clay, and stone, this would eliminate trace sources.

Even if high frequencies and certain consonants of speech that have a strong inflection and in the belief of trace elements being embedded onto the surface, time and environmental conditions would dissipate any traces of 'sound' on artifacts. The debate regarding archaeoacoustics is on-going and it still remains unspecified. To invite the question, is there another element beyond sound that may reveal the answer regarding devices similar to the "chronovisor."

DIMENSIONAL SLIPS

ANTARCTIC CASE
[Part transcript from Olga Zharina]

In March 2005, according to an article in the Russian newspaper Pravda discovered that a team of U.S scientists that were part of a government environmental project to monitor designated locations around the South Pole. One of the possible reasons for the expedition was to revisit a site and to review an incident that occurred at a secret location ten years earlier.

In 1995, a team of American and British scientists were carrying out environmental surveys across designated sections around the South Pole, but by chance, they may have discovered a time portal.

As the scientists were conducting experiments at an undisclosed location, a strange patch of grey fog suddenly appeared. As they moved closer to the anomaly, the scientist noticed that within the grey fog was a spinning vortex, which appeared to extend and move upwards into the sky, and were unable to provide details on how far or how high it went. One of the team members, US physicist Mariann McLein described the anomaly as being similar to a sandstorm. The spinning fog began to slow down, eventually coming to a complete stop. While it remained static, this provided the opportunity to probe the anomaly. Mariann McLein stated 'we have to find out what exactly we are dealing with'. The team sent up a weather balloon containing monitoring equipment that was secured to a rope; they also made sure that the balloon was close to the centre of the portal, while the researchers kept a safe distance from the anomaly. They watched cautiously as the balloon re-emerged and landed. Then by allowing a fifteen-minute interval, the team retrieved the monitoring device.

DIMENSIONAL SLIPS

They were stunned while examining the display on the chronometer, which revealed the date 27, January 1965 - exactly thirty years ago. By testing the instruments making sure factors such as the sub-zero conditions might contribute to the irregularity, the team confirmed the equipment was in working order. By continuing to repeat the experiment and by replicating the same pattern by launching the balloon and chronometer into the exact point of entry. They repeated the series of experiments several times. The results were startling each time they retrieved the chronometer; the date went back even further. The team were delegating on what steps they should take in reporting this strange occurrence.

The scientists agreed to notify the appropriate department relating to their section. At a later stage, the report of the phenomenon highlighted that it could be some form of magnetic time tunnel.

The details were dispatched to a scientific section based in the White House and documented the report under the name of "Time Gate."

Even to date, the investigation of the unusual phenomenon is still ongoing. Satellite pictures have found a whirl crater located on the South Pole, some claim it could be a tunnel to other timelines.

The CIA and the FBI are fighting to gain control over the project, as this discovery may even change the course of history. It has been suggested that further experiments will be implemented, but
it is not clear when the US federal authorities will approve of an experiment. Later in April 2001, a spy satellite was in orbit over the same location as the "Time Gate incident." High volumes of images were taken from the satellite that were later downlinked and examined by another Antarctic research team. On close examination of the images revealed a series of unexplained shapes of what might be a fabricated structure buried under the ice at an estimated depth of 3.21 kilometres (2miles).

Close to the time-gate vortex is Lake Vostok, located on the eastern part of Antarctica, an expansive subglacial lake believed to be 14 million years old. Previously in 1990, Russian mineral teams were test-drilling sections of Lake Vostok, and were "advised" by a monitoring authority (not specified) to cease work on that location until further notice due to potential eco hazards.

Later in 1998, the project was permanently shut down. There have been reports of strange incidents and anomalies around this region over the past few years.

These threads of information regarding anomalies led to a media blackout, also to discourage any more scientific investigations, as the National Security Agency (NSA) took control of the area under their authority. The location has been sealed off to the media and even to scientists due to "environmental concerns." The NSA highlighted the justification by emphasising it is an "environmentally hazardous site." Moreover, the media blackout was enforced, due to the discovery of a powerful magnetic field located at the northern section of the lake.

According to a report by the e-newspaper, Antarctic Sun outlined that during an aerial survey carried out by a Support Officer for Aerophysical Research or SOAR, conducted a magnetic resonance survey of the area. He discovered startling readings of 1,000 to 60,000 nT *, which would be considered as abnormal. The expected range prior to testing the magnetic reading should have been expected to be around 500 to 600 nT*. Being that there is a possible hidden structure in the location, moreover the structure may be linked to powerful magnetic anomalies.

This discovery according to online media sources created a clash of opinions over the nature of this remote location. One of the prime factors of the spinning fog case could be that the high magnetic presence is part of the residual transmissions of the unknown structure.

[* Nanoteslas= nT are a measurement of magnetic fields]

RUSSIAN TIME TRAVEL EXPERIMENTS

"Famous Russian scientist Nikolay Kozyrev conducted an experiment to prove that moving from the future to the past was possible. He substantiated his views with the hypotheses on instant information spreading through physical characteristics of time. Nikolay Kozyrev even supposed that 'time could execute the work and produce energy.' An American physics theorist has arrived at the conclusion that time is what existed before the existence of the world. It is known that each of us feels a different course of time under different conditions. Once a mountain climber described the moment when he was struck by lightning, describing how he saw the lightning penetrating his arm, slowly moving along it, gradually separating the skin from the tissues, and carbonizing his cells. He felt as if there were quills of thousands hedgehogs under his skin. "Russian writer Gennady Belimov was also an investigator of anomalous phenomena, philosopher, and author of numerous books. He once published an article under the headline "Time Machine: First Speed On" in the newspaper *On the Verge of Impossible.* He described how in 1987, unique experiments conducted by a group of enthusiasts led by Dr Vadim Chernobrov, launched the creation of time machines, which used methods such as "electromagnetic pumping". The experiments continued up until 2001, Vadim Chernobrov's team could slow down or speed up the course of time by modifying the magnetic field.

The biggest slowing down of time made up 1.5 seconds within an hour of the equipment's operation in labs. In August 2001, a new model of the time machine meant for a human was set in a remote forest in Russia's Volgograd Region. The device could even be activated using car batteries with a low capacity; it still accomplished to alter a fraction of time by three per cent; the change was registered with symmetrical crystal oscillators.

At first, the researchers spent five, ten, and twenty minutes in the operating machine, the longest stay lasted for half an hour. Vadim Chernobrov said that the people felt as if they moved to a different world; they felt life here and "there" at the same time as if some space was unfolding. "I cannot define the unusual feelings that we experienced at such moments." [*22]

Russian Time Travel Research: The Beginnings

Gennady Belimov says the Russian president was not informed of Vadim Chernobrov's experiment, however, he tells that even under Stalin there was a Research Institute of the Parallel World.

Results of experiments conducted by academicians Igor Kurchatov and Abram Ioffe can be found in the archives. In 1952, the head of Soviet secret police organization, Lavrenty Beria initiated a case against the researchers who participated in the experiments, as a result, 18 professors were executed by shooting, and 59 candidates including doctors of physical sciences were sent to camps.

The Institute recommenced its activity under Khrushchev. However, an experimental stand with eight leading researchers disappeared in 1961, and buildings close to the one where experiments that took place were abandoned. After that, the Communist Party political bureau and the Council of Ministers decided to suspend researchers of the institute for an uncertain period.[*23].

Dr Vadim Chernobnov (1966-2017)

One of the pioneers of time travel experiments in Russia was Dr Vadim Chernobnov who initiated experiments in 1986-7.

He was part of the Moscow's Aviation Institute UFO research team in the spacecraft department, or Kosmopoisk.

At a later stage, he decided to develop a prototype device for time-travel. However, he knew this proposal would be rejected for state funding so he rebranded the prototype model not as a time machine but as a "Prospective Space Transportation System (PSTS) to avoid ridicule." Dr Chernobnov began constructing a prototype device, an orb shaped object slightly smaller than a football that was layered by electromagnetic "skins." The internal structure consisted of a mesh of wires and several small clocks; the output wire was connected to an electrical transformer. Dr Chernobov indicated that the Prospective Space Transportation System could control time rates.

In one of his tests, he compared that every 3,600 seconds outside of the structure would be 40 seconds slower inside the PSTS module, giving a reading of 3,560 seconds. Dr Chernobov concluded that electromagnetic fields, though slight, could alter the passage of time. The extensive aspect of the research began in 1986, followed by his first lab experiment in 1987.

One of the core components of his experiment was to use "electromagnetic pumping." The method was to induce a localised field with powerful electromagnetic energy. As the electromagnetic energy resonates around the capsule, this produces a slight curve in gravity, eventually affecting the ambient (or surrounding) natural magnetic field. While conducting the first experiment in 1987, the result was that the scientists succeeded in slowing down of time to 1.5 seconds after one hour of operation. In later experiments, chronometers were installed; additional checks included calibrating the device before the field is energised.

THREADS OF TIME

The participant is placed inside the capsule; in the first phase, the team used insects; they died within a few minutes.

The second phase, lab mice were used, as most of them died at alternating stages. The cause of death with the lab mice was due to different parts of the body, being affected by the varied acceleration points. In the third test, a puppy was used. It was placed in the pod for 108 minutes; the puppy survived, but behaved as if he was having rabies. A few human volunteers who were brave enough took part in the second experiment with two participants. The results were a divergence of time by 1.5 seconds or translated as a 3% shift in time.

A revision of the experiment was conducted in 1996, electromagnets were installed in the base of the device [approximately 1meter in diameter], these elements were layered on top of each other. A sequence of powerful electric pulses were inputted into the unit and formed to focus the energy into the central section of the module.

The Experiment

The time travel experiment was relaunched, as by now the political landscape in Russia was changing compared to the previous government constraints. Resuming its activity the Research of the Parallel Worlds relaunched the experiments in 1989. They searched for a site and chose a remote location in the Anzhu Islands, situated between the Laptev Sea and the East Siberian Sea. Eventually setting up a laboratory, they began to proceed with the experiment on the 780-ton time-travel module. On the 30th of August 1989, an enormous explosion occurred at the laboratory, which destroyed 2.5 square kilometres of the surrounding area, also killing three of the scientists who were inside the module. A message was sent from the team as the experiment was in progress; a transmission came through 'We are dying, but keep on with the experiment'. It is very dark here. All objects are double, our limbs are transparent, the oxygen supply-will only last 43 hours and the life support system is damaged. 'We don't know what is happening, send a message to our loved ones-I think we are going to die'.

Later, Olga Zharina wrote about the occurrence for Pravda, which incidentally, did not fully emerge in the European and US features until five years later. It is believed that the scientist may have traversed into an alternate location and may have collided with an unknown element that damaged their power units causing them to be marooned within another dimension. Moreover, they could have entered a portal in space and collided with a meteorite. The main site for the experiment was located in a remote forest as the illustration. One of the pods was fabricated from papier-mache. The dimensions would have been 1 meter in diameter and 1.7 meters in height. This pod in the second stage of testing would have used small animals. Later in 2001, an updated version of the "time machine" was developed for human subjects who were eager and confident to be part of the experiment.

The designated location for the next stage was a remote forest in the Volgograd region, situated in Russia's Southern Federal District. The power supply to the apparatus was modified, so that it could be operated by using an array of 12v car batteries, and by having low capacity, it still could alter the reversal by 3%. The results were recorded using crystal oscillators. The primary components consisted of a sequence of electromagnets; the internal section contained several small clocks that were connected to a transformer, quartz generators, fibre- optic laser diodes and an array of wires. Three researchers entered the pod, some varied the time by staying for 5-10 minutes. One researcher spent 30 minutes in the cramped device, he described the experience of 'feeling detached, as if time and space were unfolding'. No other reports on whether this time machine was still conducting experiments beyond 2001.

Olga Zharina.

THE PLANE THAT VANISHED

By Tara MacIsaac

In 1969, a 747 National Airlines flight from Miami was preparing to land at Washington National Airport (Now known as Ronald Reagan Washington National Airport). As the plane approached the runway, and flying at an altitude of approximately 500 feet, suddenly vanished.

At this height, the aircraft would have been visible to anyone on the ground, and been easily detected by air traffic control.

Emergency crews were alerted on the assumption that the plane had somehow gone off course and crashed near the airport.

Emergency vehicles gathered on the runway where the plane was last seen. Ten minutes had passed; suddenly the plane reappeared in the precise location it had vanished. The clocks on the plane, including passengers' watches, were all 10 minutes behind. To the passengers on the plane, those ten minutes had never passed. While looking out on the runway as the plane made its descent, it seemed to everyone on board, the emergency vehicles just appeared out of thin air.

Martin Caidin (1927–1997) investigated this purported incident. Caidin was an aviation and aeronautics expert who was frequently consulted by NASA for his extensive knowledge of the space agency's history. He was also a science fiction writer; one of his most famous works was "Cyborg," which was later adapted for television as "The Six Million Dollar Man." As the plane commenced its approach towards the runway, it disappeared, as described 'literally into thin air' Later in an unpublished account, Martin Caidin outlined the incident he also highlighted as "Men in Suits" a dissimilar variant to "Men in Black" just turned up out of nowhere. Later as the plane landed the "men in suits" filed onto the plane and took control of the situation, then rumours began to circulate that this particular aircraft was targeted for some sort of interdimensional experiment.[*24]

Thanks to Julia Ries - The Epoch Times for the use of the article.

DIMENSIONAL SLIPS

SEVILLE, SPAIN

Interdimensional slip

The following case would-be described as a possible multiversal teleportation incident, which happened near the town of Alcalá de Guadaíra, located 10 kilometres from Seville.

A journalist who interviewed Mr Ramirez about his experience, described him as 'a rational and highly educated person'. Pedro Ramirez, who by profession is an engineer also mentioned when he was 17 years old, he experienced a succession of strange events; one included an encounter with a UFO. It was at approximately 11:00PM on the 9th November 1986; Pedro Ramirez was driving from work and heading towards his home in Alcalá de Guadaíra. He knows this route automatically with every passing detail, even the small side-tracks and buildings along the way. While trailing the curve on the road, he suddenly found himself in a strange looking environment. Bewildered and shocked to find a busy six-lane highway, surrounded by peculiar looking landscape and structures. The buildings were also strange, describing them as being 20 storeys high and made of glass, with additional curious looking small houses.

Another strange detail, the other cars along the highway were also out of place. They were the type of cars still used in Cuba; the old-fashioned Cadillac's from the 1950's.

'He noticed the other vehicles passing him with a frequency – or at intervals – of 8 minutes between one and the other. He kept driving for another hour, then stopped again and got out for another quarter of an hour'. 'The cars only had two colours either white or beige, they also had peculiar licence plates unlike the one issued in Spain. He described the plates as unmarked dark rectangles. As Ramirez continued driving he began to experience, strange background sounds of what he described as a 'chorus of voices singing'.

It was then a voice spoke to him- transmitting a fragmented message 'You have been teleported' uncertain on whether it was an actual voice or a telepathic message. One prominent detail was the heat; the temperature was unusual for this time of year. Eventually he arrived at some crossroads, which he had never seen before. There was a signpost giving directions to Alcalá, Malaga, and Seville. He continued towards Alcalá, however, within a few minutes he was driving along the road that led to his house.

The whole experience seemed to last about half an hour, however he noticed what would have been a journey of about forty minutes lasted three hours. The following day Mr Ramirez retraced the journey and found there were no crossroads or road signs and no sign of a six-lane highway. He continued to explore the area by examining a series of maps covering his route from Seville to Alcalá de Guadaíra, but was unable to find anything significant.

Courtesy of S. Corrales Inexplicata-the journal of Hispanic ufology 29, 04, 2012]

Chelsea, London, UK.

Back in 2001, one of the members of a phenomena based forum sent this account relating to a strange experience that happened to one of his former work colleagues.

Sometime around the late 1970s, a man called R.A lived close to Beaufort Street in the district of Chelsea, west London. One Sunday morning while nipping out for a newspaper and recalled a "curious shortcut." Instead of visiting the usual shop not far from his house, he decided to go to other newsagents just off the Kings Road. It was about 10:30 am when he set off and took an alternative route through a park near Fetter Lane, which leads to a church, situated behind Beaufort Street. It was about early September when the weather forecast predicted a thunderstorm, R.A commented 'I remember deep grey metallic looking clouds were building up, and thinking I better hurry up before I get soaked.' As he continued to walk across the park and into the side street, he noticed how unusually quiet it was. R.A commented that 'even around here, you should be able to hear noise from the traffic, after all London never stops'. As he continued to walk, he began to feel mild electric shocks, which seemed to spiral down from the top of his head then all the way to the tips of his fingers. Impulsively, he looked above him thinking 'Where did that come from?' Moments later, he caught the odour of what smelt like a leaky TV set, or as he reflected an overworked Xerox™ machine at the office. He added 'That smell of static electricity suddenly drifted across the path.' As he looked behind him, usually there would be a row of houses and 1930s type flats; 'they just seemed to have vanished, just a grey space as if fog had suddenly appeared.'

The most peculiar thing he noticed was the pavement. It was not the usual asphalt and the standard sections of concrete paving. While taking a glance at the road surface, he noticed a metallic shimmer, a continuous strip of grey metal that also emitted a smell of static electricity. Taking a second glance, R.A noticed the familiar buildings and houses in front of him were gone.

Now confused and in a state of panic 'What the heck is going on?' was his first response but carried on with his intended route. 'Despite everything having a weird smell, and peculiar silence, I began to lose my bearings.' 'Did I fall over and knock myself out?' all these thoughts wove through my mind'. A tingling sensation began to build up, as he glanced to his left, he noticed curious looking buildings.

Unusual looking structures propped up on columns, deep blue triangular-shaped buildings, in which one side of a building was coated with a reflected material.

He added, 'I used to look at future development projects in the town planning demonstrations, but I couldn't relate to any of the designs I saw.' As he looked at his watch, he noticed the second swipe hand had stopped. While glancing around the street and at the curious buildings, a Morris Marina car whizzed past him, it appeared "regular." Relieved, realising he was back to normal as the metallic road suddenly vanished. He noticed the usual concrete pavements, and the familiar looking buildings had returned so he continued walking towards the road junction. The immediate response was to look at his watch; it displayed 11:30 am. However, he set off at 9:00 AM; the distance to the newsagents was just a ten-minute walk, hardly even a mile. It appeared that he had an unaccountable lapse of an hour and half, 'what happened?

A week later on Sunday R.A attempted to see if he could experience the "slip" again. Repeating the same route, he set off at the exact time as he did the previous week, but nothing happened. He carried out some research in the library, reading books on London-based unexplained files especially around Chelsea, examining maps from the earliest to the most recent; to see if anything might enable a link to strange phenomena.

The only possible explanation could be the primary geological profile that consists of alluvium- clay, bedrock London clay formation, and no evidence of geological fault lines. As regarding geological factors, nothing suggests a potential medium for creating a localised anomaly.

DID THE LARGE HADRON COLLIDER CREATE TIME TRAVEL?
Machine shut down after plane vanishes'
By Jon Austin Daily Express.

THE Large Hadron Collider "created a 'time warp' that sent a passenger jet thousands of miles off course" in the blink of an eye and caused a massive power blackout, it has shockingly been claimed. The huge scientific experiment, which is used to collide particles to discover more about how the universe formed, opened a time portal meaning an Iberworld Airbus A330-300 ended up landing 5,500 miles from where it was supposed to, conspiracy theorists say. Built among miles of tunnels under the Swiss-French border, the complex machine is run by the European Organisation for Nuclear Research (CERN)

Claims now ride that CERN scientists shut down the LHC during an experiment immediately after the incident with the plane. An article on website Freedom Fighter Times said: "The power released from the LHC was so strong that it sent a time warp across the planet.

"What really happened can best be explained as a massive power outage all across South America." The report said CERN scientists began a series of experiments during which they discovered their testing was "distorting our Earth's magnetic field and had 'shot off' a 'time wave' towards the core of the planet". Tracking showed the wave veered exactly towards the 'Sun Gate' high in the Bolivian Andes mountains, the report said. The report added the "initial 'time wave' spawned by the LHC" erupted from the 'Sun Gate' and headed out towards the space above South America.

The wave then "skimmed into the path of an Iberworld Airbus A330-300 flown by Air Comet which was ready to begin its descent into Santa Cruz, Bolivia, but then found itself 'instantly and mysteriously' over the skies of Santa Cruz, in Tenerife, Spain, over 5,500 miles away".

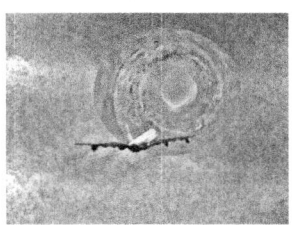

All 170 passengers and the crew of flight A7-301 were safe, and after 17 hours on the ground in Spain the departed back to Bolivia. The bizarre plane incident is said to have happened on November 1 2009.

.A day later CERN lost power at the LHC and announced some days later in a statement a bird had dropped a piece of baguette onto the machinery, causing the shutdown. The report added: "After this mysterious event CERN scientists shut down the LHC blaming their failed experiment on a bird dropping a piece of bread onto outdoor machinery. "After which their Director for Research and Scientific- Computing, Sergio Bertolucci, warned that the titanic LHC machine may possibly create or discover previously unimagined scientific phenomena, or 'unknown unknowns' such as an 'extra dimension'". The report, and other similar ones went onto claim, even after the LHC was shut down, "dimensional distortions" created in South America by the "time wave" continued and caused the Gateway of the Sun monolith to send out what Russian scientists likened to a "digital communication." This was said to have been blasted towards thousands of Pyramids and other ancient sites in Brazil and the Andes Region, leading to a massive power outage plunging "tens-of-millions of people into darkness". So is any of this true? Well it is true that CERN had been testing the LHC on November 1, after it was out of action for more than a year, following a previous power failure however, there was no suggestion in these reports of any time anomalies.

But the cause of this was given as a huge hydroelectric dam began suddenly malfunctioning. The Itaipu dam, across the two borders stopped producing 17,000 megawatts of power.

The cause was not determined at the time, but was thought to be strong storms uprooting trees near the dam.

"The power released from the LHC was so strong that it sent a time warp across the planet. What really happened can best be explained as a massive power outage all across South America." Freedom Fighter Times.' Sceptics say conspiracy theorists are very good at filling in blanks and joining dots. They also monitor news sites, so when events like these occur around the same time; they piece them together to create a new theory. This, coupled with a distrust of most official explanations for unexpected events, means there is only going to be one outcome and a theory is born which then travels like wildfire over various websites, debunkers claim. According to the neutral howitworks.com website, it is easy for the theories to begin and travel. A report on the website said: "For a conspiracy theory to get started there has to be something that a conspiracy theorist can use, something that doesn't make sense. In some conspiracy theories, it's something very small. "Cosmic rays – particles produced by events in outer space – collide with particles in the Earth's atmosphere at much greater energies than those of the LHC. These cosmic rays have been bombarding the Earth's atmosphere as well as other astronomical bodies since these bodies were formed, with no harmful consequences.

"These planets and stars have stayed intact despite these higher energy collisions over billions of years." CERN said: 'The LHC will not generate black holes in the cosmological sense.

'However, some theories suggest that the formation of tiny 'quantum' black holes may be possible. 'The observation of such an event would be thrilling in terms of our understanding of the Universe; and would be perfectly safe'.

THE PHILADELPHIA EXPERIMENT

There have been 64 books and 2 films made about this alleged top-secret government experiment, moreover, also the recipient of constant debunking. However, the incident continues to retain curiosity as elements of what was considered a top-secret project are within the realms of time slips and interdimensional transference. This is a brief overview of the experiment, as going into the complete version of the account would become an entire book in itself.

There are two versions of how the Philadelphia Experiment occurred; nevertheless, it was decades later when the full details of the incident began to filter into the mainstream media. One version begins, when two sailors on shore leave, were sitting on a park bench in New York. Moments later, a haggard looking man sits next to them. The man looked at the sailors, and began to start a conversation with the usual dialogue and pleasantries. Eventually opening up and telling them how he served in the Navy during World War II.

Three of them swapped stories, comparing places they went to etc. Pausing for a moment, the haggard looking man said: 'I'll have a story that you will never believe'. He told them what happened while on board a ship in 1943. He also highlighted on being part of a bizarre secret weapons experiment and how a 360-foot destroyer vanished into thin air. *[JPH]*

A Dr. Franklin Reno (or Rinehart) conducted the experiment as a military application of the Unified Field Theory. The concept briefly postulates the interconnected nature of the forces that comprise electromagnetic radiation and gravity. Through a separate application of the theory, it was thought possible, with specialized equipment and sufficient energy, to bend light around an object in such a way as to render it essentially invisible to observers.

The Navy considered this application of the theory to be of obvious military value (especially as the United States was engaged in World War II at the time) and both approved and sponsored the experiment. A navy destroyer escort, the USS Eldridge, was fitted with the required equipment at the naval yards in Philadelphia. [*25]

Testing began in summer 1943, and was successful to a limited degree. One test, on July 22, resulted in the Eldridge being rendered almost completely invisible, with some witnesses reporting a "greenish fog" in its place. However, crewmembers complained of severe nausea afterwards. At that point, the experiment was altered at the request of the Navy, with the new objective being invisible to radar only. The equipment was not correctly re-calibrated to this end, but in spite of this, the experiment was performed again on October 28. This time, Eldridge not only became almost entirely invisible to the naked eye, but also vanished from the area in a flash of blue light. Simultaneously, the US naval base at Norfolk, Virginia, just over 600 km (375 miles) away, reported sighting the Eldridge offshore for several minutes, whereupon the Eldridge vanished from their sight and reappeared in Philadelphia, at the point it had originally occupied in an apparent case of accidental teleportation. The physiological effects on the crew were profound. Almost all of the crew were violently ill, while others because of their experience suffered from mental illness including the behaviour consistent with schizophrenia. Others claimed that five of the crew were fused to the metal sections of the ship; witnesses also claim that some of the men began to fade in and out, and then disappear. Horrified by these results, navy officials immediately cancelled the experiment.

All of the surviving crew involved were discharged; in some accounts, brainwashing techniques were employed in an attempt to make the remaining crew members lose their memories of the experience. In 1955, Morris K. Jessup, an amateur astronomer and former graduate-level researcher, published *The Case for the UFO*, a book about unidentified flying objects, which contained some theorizing about the means of propulsion that flying-saucer-style UFOs might use. Jessup speculated that anti-gravity and/or manipulation of electromagnetism might be the process for the flight behaviour of UFOs as described in reported cases. concentrated in the area of rocketry, and that little attention was paid to these other theoretical means of flight, which he felt would ultimately be more fruitful. [*26]

On January 13, 1955, Jessup received a letter from a man identifying himself as Carlos Allende. In the letter, Allende informed Jessup of the Philadelphia Experiment, alluding to poorly sourced contemporary newspaper articles as proof. Allende also said that he had witnessed the Eldridge disappear and reappear while serving aboard the liberty cargo ship SS Andrew Furuseth. Allende also named other crew members who served aboard the Andrew Furuseth, and claimed to know of the fates of some of the crew of the Eldridge after the experiment, including one whom he witnessed disappear during a chaotic fight in a bar. Jessup replied to Allende by postcard, asking for further evidence and corroboration for the story. The reply came months later; however, this time the correspondent identified himself as Carl M Allen.

Allen said that he could not provide the details for which Jessup was asking, but implied that he might be able to recall by means of hypnosis. Suspecting that Allende/Allen was a crank, Jessup decided to discontinue the correspondence.

In the spring of 1957, Jessup was contacted by the Office of Naval Research (ONR) in Washington, D.C. and asked to study the contents of a parcel that they had received. Upon arrival, a curious Jessup was astonished to find that a paperback copy of his UFO book had been mailed to ONR in a manila envelope marked "Happy Easter." Further, the book had been extensively annotated by hand in its margins, and an ONR officer asked Jessup if he had any idea as to who had done so. The lengthy annotations were written in three different colours of ink, and appeared to detail a correspondence between three individuals, only one of which is given a name: "Jemi." The ONR labelled the other two "Mr A" and "Mr B." The annotators refer to each other as "Gypsies," and discuss two different types of "people" living in outer space.

Their text contained nonstandard use of capitalization and punctuation, and detailed a lengthy discussion of the merits of various suppositions that Jessup makes throughout his book, with oblique references to the Philadelphia Experiment, in a way that suggested prior or superior knowledge. [*26]

Based on the handwriting style and subject matter, Jessup identified "Mr A" as Allende/Allen. Others have suggested that the three annotations are actually from the same person, using three pens. A transcription of the annotated "Varo edition" is available online, complete with three-color notes.

Later, the ONR contacted Jessup, claiming that the return address on Allende's letter to Jessup was an abandoned farmhouse. They also informed Jessup that the Varo Corporation, a research firm, was preparing a print copy of the annotated version of The Case for the UFO, complete with both letters he had received. About a hundred copies of the Varo Edition were printed and distributed within the Navy. Jessup was also sent three for his own use.

Jessup attempted to make a living writing on the topic, but his follow-up book did not sell well and his publisher rejected several other manuscripts. In 1958, his wife left him, and friends described him as being depressed and somewhat unstable when he travelled to New York. After returning to Florida he was involved in a serious car accident and was slow to recover, apparently increasing his despondency. Morris Jessup committed suicide in 1959. In 1965, Vincent Gaddis published Invisible Horizons: True Mysteries of the Sea, in which the story of the experiment from the Varo annotation is recounted. Later, in 1977, Charles Berlitz, an author of several books on paranormal phenomena, included a chapter on the experiment in his book *Without a Trace: New Information from the Triangle.*

In 1978, a novel, *Thin Air* by George E Simpson and Neal R Burger was released. This was a dramatic fictional account, clearly inspired by the foregoing works, of a conspiracy to cover up an horrific experiment gone wrong on board the Eldridge in 1943. In 1979, Berlitz and a co-author, William L. Moore, published *The Philadelphia Experiment:*

Project Invisibility, the best known and most cited source of information about the experiment to date. [*26] In 1984, the story was eventually adapted into a motion picture, The Philadelphia Experiment directed by Stewart Rafill. Though based only loosely on prior accounts of the experiment, it served to bring the core elements of the original story into mainstream scrutiny.

In 1990, Alfred Bielek, a self-claimed former crew-member of the Eldridge and alleged witness of the experiment, supported the version as it was
portrayed in the movie, adding embellishments, which were disseminated via the internet, eventually to surface in various mainstream outlets. In 2003, a small team of investigators debunked Bielek's version of his participation in the Philadelphia Experiment, and the consensus now is that he was nowhere near the ship at the proposed time of the experiment.

Many observers argue it inappropriate to put much credence in an unusual story put forward by one individual, in the absence of more conclusive corroborating evidence. An article written by Robert Goerman for Fate in 1980 claimed that Carlos Allende aka Carl Allen was in fact Carl Meredith Allen of New Kensington, Pennsylvania, who had an established psychiatric history and may have fabricated the primary history of the experiment as a result of his illness.-In particular, is stark in illustrating the near-total lack of research by those who eventually publicized the story. Others speculate that much of the key literature has more emphasis on dramatic embellishment rather than pertinent research. Though Berlitz and Moore's famous account of the story (The Philadelphia Experiment: Project Invisibility) contained much supposedly factual information, such as transcripts of an interview with a scientist involved in the experiment.

It has also been criticized for plagiarizing key story elements from the fictitious novel *Thin Air* published a year earlier, which, it is argued, undermines the credibility of the text as a whole. [*26]

THE PHILADELPHIA EXPERIMENT

Scientific Aspects

Albert Einstein never fully developed his Unified Field Theory, and no consistent UFT or gravity-electromagnetism link has since come forth from the scientific community. Though Nikola Tesla claimed to have completed a Unified Field Theory project shortly before his death in 1943, his theories on electromagnetism's power to distort space and time were never published. Conspiracy theorists propose that the FBI promptly following his death seized most of Tesla's research papers, and highlight the apparent coincidence between the year of his death and the supposed date of the Philadelphia Experiment. More recent research, such as at Duke University demonstrates clearly that, even in 2006, the scientific community was far from attaining the level of technology required to render invisible an object the size of a naval destroyer.

Timeline Inconsistencies

The USS Eldridge was not commissioned until August 27, 1943, and remained in port in New York City until September 1943. The October experiment allegedly took place while the ship was on its first shakedown cruise in the Bahamas. A reunion of veterans who served aboard the Eldridge told the Philadelphia Inquirer in April 1999 that the ship had never made port in Philadelphia. Further evidence against the Philadelphia experiment timeline comes from the USS Eldridge's complete WWII action report, including the remarks section of the 1943 deck log, available on microfilm.[*26] The project team did not expect this added teleportation from the shipyard in Philadelphia to Norfolk. As the generator was activated and the extreme high voltage was fed into the coils the Eldridge vanished- and the result seemed to be successful. However, as the Eldridge returned, now covered in a green haze, this was a result of the coils. When activated, the coils generated a powerful electrical field, gradually heating up the surrounding air and water, and creating localised evaporation that surrounded the USS Eldrige, with a blanket of green mist.

The team watched in horror as the men jumped into the water most of the men were covered in flames, some had their limbs embedded into the bulkhead, and others were partially melded into the floor and the hull. [*26]

In a later report outlined, that some of the men might have ended up into another dimension or even forty years into the future.

One or two of the survivors of the event described what happened while on board, how some of the fellow crew members were walking through solid walls, and as they returned some were stuck in between solid structures, and others just vanished into thin air...

Alternative Explanations

[*26] Present day scientists propose that the generators rigged to the ship may not have been designed to warp space/time. Instead, they could have been deployed to heat up the air and water around the ship, creating an artificial mirage, thereby rendering the ship "invisible" to the human eye. Alternatively, researcher Jacques Vallee describes a procedure on board the USS Engstrom, which was docked alongside the Eldridge in 1943. The operation involved the generation of a powerful electromagnetic field on board the ship in order to degauss it, with the goal of rendering the ship undetectable to magnetically triggered torpedoes and mines. A Canadian engineer invented this system, and the British used it widely during the Second World War. [*26]

THE PHILADELPHIA EXPERIMENT

British ships of the era often included such systems built-in on the upper decks (the conduits are still visible on the deck of the HMS Belfast in London). Degaussing is still used today; however, it has no effect on visible light or radar. Vallee speculates that the accounts of Engstrom's degaussing may have been garbled in subsequent retellings, and these accounts may have influenced the story of the Philadelphia Experiment.

A veteran who served on board the Engstrom noted that the Eldridge could have indeed travelled from Philadelphia to Norfolk and back again in a single day at a time when merchant ships could not have access to the Chesapeake and Delaware Canal, which at the time was only open to naval vessels. Use of this channel was kept silent: German submarines had recently been ravaging East Coast shipping during Operation Drumbeat, and thus military ships unable to protect themselves were secretly moved via canals to avoid this threat.

It should be noted that the same veteran claims to be the man whom Allende witnessed "disappear" at a bar. He claims that when the fight broke out, friendly barmaids whisked him out the back door of the bar before the police arrived, because he was under age. They then covered for him by claiming that he disappeared.

In a more speculative and strongly paranormal vein, AL Bielek and Duncan Cameron both claim to have leapt from the deck of the Eldridge while it was in "hyperspace" between Philadelphia and Norfolk. They ended up, after a period of severe disorientation, at the Air Force station Montauk Point, Long Island in 1983, having experienced not only teleportation but time travel.

They claim John von Neumann met them there (although officially he died in 1957). This story is part of a continuum involving another alleged secret US Government experiment into the paranormal known as the Montauk Project.[*26]

Kind permission from Ellie Crystal Website: www.crystalinks.com

DIE GLOCKE; HITLER'S TIME MACHINE

In 1997 a journalist called, Igor Witowski uncovered one of the most top-secret projects initiated by Nazi scientists. Witowski also managed to acquire classified Polish Government documents from an unnamed Polish intelligence officer, who extracted the details of the experiment while interrogating a former SS Obergruppenfuhrer Jakob Sporrenberg, responsible for war crimes committed in Poland and the Soviet Union. Originally held by the War Crimes Integration Unit in London, Sporrenberg was later extradited to Poland in 1946. He gave full details and access to files on a range of top secret and if not bizarre Nazi projects.

Sections of the disclosed files included documents that contained details and plans of a device called Die Glocke or The Bell.

[*27] Die Glocke, was going to be one of the collection of "WunderWaffe" or "Wonder Weapons," of the Nazi regime.

The lab facility was situated deep within a vast network of tunnels located on the outskirts of Ludwikowice, Lower Silesia.

Die Glock: fabricated using specialised hardened steel, it was 3 meters (9 ft.) wide and 4 to 5 meters (12 to 15 ft.) high, the design resembled the shape of a bell, hence the name Die Glocke or the English translation The Bell. Etched on the base, were a series of lines and glyphs, which could have been Old Germanic runic markings.

The original idea for the design was developed in 1943 at a facility in Hamburg. One of the team who created the device was the Norwegian physicist Rolf Wideroe, who specialised in particle acceleration. Known as the betatron experiment, the main aspect of his research included the method of using resonating particles by applying a radio frequency combined with an electromagnetic field.

In the post war years, Wideroe was active in the development of particle accelerators and in 1952 collaborated with CERN, which included directing preliminary studies for the proton synchrotron projects. Wideroe kept a documented account of the experiment while working for a company called CHF Muller.

Technical details contained within the documents included how the device generated a powerful magnetic field. In addition, the results described the tests on a prototype sphere that was contained inside another sphere, which spun on an axle when activated. The prototype led to the next phase, a sealed unit was applied to create a vacuum; this aided the production of ionised gas called plasma, additionally mercury was also included in the solution, which played a role by releasing photons into the plasma.

The completed structure consisted of two rotating cylinders; these cylinders contained a mercury substitute called Xerum 525, described as purple or red in colour. A compound of paraffin, beryllium, and thorium peroxide, the paraffin element was applied as a moderator, as used in previous reactor experiments.

This purple liquid was injected into the central section from flasks attached to the side of the device. Paraffin along with a compound of deuterium (heavy hydrogen) would have the role of stabilizing fast particles. An additional new material called 'Leichtmetall' or "light metal" may have been part of the Die Glocke's structure. During the operation, scientists suffered from sleep deprivation, dizziness and some even died due to radiation poisoning....

[*27] 'Although no evidence of the accuracy of Witkowski's statements have been produced, they reached a wider audience when they were retold by British author Nick Cook, who added his own views to Witkowski's statements in *The Hunt for Zero Point* '[*27]

How did it work?

When initiated, the two internal cylinders would rotate at high speed, while the build-up of acceleration would generate a collision of photons and electrons, thus creating radiation, and the release of thermal neutrons. The mercury component would generate ionised plasma; the plasma circulated around the axle that was set within a controlled frequency.

As the device was running, it could generate millions of volts, creating an electromagnetic vortex. So powerful, the vortex could generate anti-gravity.

Other publications indicate that the scheme known as Project "Riese" (Giant) was part of a nuclear weapons program. However, other sources speculate that it was a propulsion system for experimental aircraft; it may have been used for anti-gravity experiments.

Close to the town of Ludwikowice, stands a decagonal shaped concrete structure dubbed "The Henge." The function of this concrete frame may have been an unfinished cooling tower. Others speculate that it was a test rig for the anti – gravity experiments, to stabilise the craft and to amplify energy. Also uncovered in the same location were remnants of a metal alloy frame.

However, according to additional reports, a concave mirror was installed on top of the device. Which invites the question, was the mirror used as some sort of chronovisor, for observing other dimensions, and other timelines?

Could it be that Nazi scientist had the additional notion of accessing other dimensions or future timelines for advanced weaponry? Other sources propose that the definitive purpose of Die Glocke was to be used as a time machine, specifying that it had the ability of creating localised wormholes.

[Wormhole: a form of channel or tunnel via space-time linking the otherwise faraway parts of the universe, wormholes work on the premise of the Einstein-Rosen Bridge principle]. According to theoretical physicist, John Weeler in 1955 stated that 'wormholes exist naturally'-

He also stipulates that 'wormholes can appear anywhere spontaneously and also disappear due to the fluctuation of spacetime even on a small scale due to quantum mechanics'.

When scientists were conducting a "cloaking experiment" using extreme high voltages [Philadelphia Experiment], according to Nikola Tesla, in one of his experiments, managed to generate a charge of 3.5 million volts by using a device he created known as the "Tesla Coil." During the process, Tesla discovered potential distortion in the localised magnetic field.

After being in contact with the resonance charge, he recorded his experience of perceiving varied sensations of being simultaneously in the past and future, and was almost nearly killed in the process. Debunkers might highlight that being exposed to a powerful electrical flux could have affected Tesla's mind into believing he travelled to another place in the form of hallucinations?

However, the idea that time and space may be altered with magnetic field distortion is still a factor with alternative researchers.

Later this prompted further studies and experiments by replicating Tesla's method of creating a "portal." Therefore, could it be that the Die Glocke was a teleportation device utilising localised wormholes generated by extreme voltages sourced by a prototype nuclear powered apparatus.

Origins and the concept of Die Glocke

There is a theory on why this arcane Nazi technology appeared to be so advanced. It began when a mysterious object crash-landed in the Black Forest, southwest of Germany close to the town of Freiburg in 1936. The crash occurred in the middle of a thunderstorm; reports claimed that it was an aircraft hit by a lightning bolt, observers kept track of where the object was going to land. Later on, thinking it was an enemy aircraft, SS troops- were deployed to the crash site. What they uncovered were the remnants of a saucer shaped object.

The troops set up a barrier and deterred any one from attempting to gain access. The SS troops immediately recovered the fragments and transported them to Wewelsberg Castle some 530 Km away, the main headquarters of the SS known as The Order of The Black Sun, Wewelsberg Castle is also linked with Nazi occult activities. A team of scientists worked on the craft to reverse engineer all of the components, finding ways of using the unknown technology to their advantage.

After the war, a number of files were uncovered by U.S troops, which included blueprints and schematics of experimental aircraft dating from 1938. One particular file contained diagrams of the Haunebu 1, which on inspection resembled a flying saucer.

The craft was 25m in diameter; and may have been one of the prototype designs for anti-gravity experiments. The creation of Die Glocke would have been part of the on-going development for an energy source; however, it appeared that while testing the device the research team at a later stage may have discovered additional capabilities. Hans Kammler a Nazi officer and engineer, was the principle creator of Die Glocke along with other advanced projects, and later appointed as director of the development. However, there are conflicting views to determine whether he was actually involved .Other reports mention that sixty personnel consisting of top German scientists, engineers, and researchers mysteriously disappeared.

What Happened to Die Glocke?

Most of the scientists who worked on the assignment were executed to erase any information of the project falling into the hands of the allied forces. Some theorists claim that Die Glocke was relocated

to a Nazi friendly South American country or alternatively to a secret base in Antarctica called New Swabia.

Others maintain that Die Glocke was projected towards the Hyades star cluster, as Nazi occultist believe the UFO, which landed in the Black Forest in 1936, had originated from the star Aldebaran located near Hyades. An alternative explanation refers to an incident that occurred in 1965 Kecksburg, Pennsylvania when an "object" crashed landed in the forest close to the town. Military personnel set up an exclusion zone, while salvaging the craft. The object had a similar structure to Die Glocke, creating the notion it may have traversed time and travelled 30 years into the future, or ending up in Pennsylvania.

The Kecksburg UFO sighting

On 9th December 1965, witnesses in at least six U.S. states and Ontario, Canada saw a large fireball hurtling across the sky.

While reports came in from Canada, Michigan, and northern Ohio, witnesses describe hot fragments falling from an object, causing grass fires as it sped across the night sky.

However, the object landed in some woods in the small town of Kecksburg, Pennsylvania, located 30 miles southeast from the city of Pittsburgh. A boy described how an object fell from the sky, abruptly landing in the middle of the woods, close to his house. He called out to his mother, who at the same time was about to call her son back inside. Both stood in the back yard watching wisps of blue smoke coming from the tree line, she decided immediately to alert the authorities.

Earlier, in the city of Pittsburgh, emergency services received a high volume of phone calls from residents describing a sonic boom or a large fiery craft zipping across the sky. Most of the witness reports to the press listed a variety of explanations that included a plane crash, errant missile test, or re-entering satellite debris.

Most of the residents in nearby towns said they felt a vibration, followed by a thud across the ground just as the craft had landed. Before the authorities arrived, volunteers from the local fire department headed off to the crash site. One group found an acorn shaped object embedded into the ground, giving a description 'It was made of metal, between 10 and 12 feet long the same size as a Volkswagen Beetle'. At the base of the acorn was a series of strange motifs, which resembled Egyptian hieroglyphics. A few hours later, military personnel arrived then began securing the site and ordered the civilians to keep away. Accompanying the military personnel were men in suits, who took charge of everything; they appeared to have a higher authority than the military.

A group of US Army engineers arrived with a flatbed truck; the object was lowered onto the main bed, strapped securely and swiftly covering the craft with a tarpaulin sheet. On enquiry, the military claimed they searched the woods but denied ever finding anything.

The local radio station was about to broadcast a news bulletin on the crash, curiously enough before going on air, the station was visited by two men who advised the station manager to 'limit the information' of the incident.

Other theories claimed that the object could have been the Soviet spacecraft Kosmos 96 Venus probe, as the craft had a similar outline and dimensions to the "acorn." The crash details of the Kosmos 96 are still listed as returning to earth on the 9th December 1965. However, the exact location of where the Kosmos 96 landed is yet to be confirmed.

Another factor, due to the size of the craft, and having a similar shape to an acorn, it did not have the same dimensions in proportion to the Kosmos 96.

Other speculations outlined that the Kecksburg UFO was a secret US Government backed project, a device used for experiments in time travel. In the final days of WW2 as the allied forces moved into Germany, may have discovered Die Glocke in a hidden location.

The U.S Military would have initiated the safeguarding of this and other devices for government scientist to reverse engineer. Speculative theories include, government backed scientists may have created a similar device developed through reverse engineering, and the outcome could have been the Kecksburg Acorn?

THE IRAQ STARGATE:

The invasion of Iraq led by U.S and coalition forces began on the 18th March 2003. The objective was to 'disarm Iraq of the weapons of mass destruction, and to end Saddam Hussein's support for terrorism, and to free the Iraqi people.' [*28] It was also claimed that Sadaam Hussein had links with Al-Qaeda, who were responsible for the 9/11 bombings in 2001. The primary motive for the invasion was to act on Iraq's failure in not complying with meeting the deadline set by the United Nations Security Council. It has been pitched around various news sites and forums that the invasion of Iraq regarding weapons of mass destruction (WMD) was a smoke screen and the actual motive could be something to do with oil. Moreover, it has been argued, there was no firm evidence for the existence of chemical weapons being stockpiled. However, another possible concealed motive could be to gain access to a device known as the "Stargate. " Which according to various sources is an ancient structure, located near Eridu, a city approximately 316 km south-east of Baghdad — the Stargate has the ability to access portals hidden within the Earth's magnetic field. Archaeological artifacts, especially depictions on a variety of objects have generated the idea that some ancient cultures, even with their limited resources, were technologically advanced. The study of ancient Mesopotamia and Sumerian culture by alternative archaeologists suggest that the ancient Sumerians could have been guided by interdimensional, ethereal, or extra-terrestrial entities that may have transferred knowledge to the human inhabitants. Alternative archaeologists, who are also known as *ancient astronaut theorists,* indicate within their research that one group of entities known as the Anunnaki, may be one of the key influencers.

THE IRAQ STARGATE:

These strange beings have been depicted on clay tablets, dating to around 2500 B.C; additional claims maintain that the presence of the Anunnaki could go back even further. In the 1920's a team of archaeologists from Europe unearthed what they believed was a series of structures in various locations around Iraq, one of the finds might have been the Stargate. However, the archaeologists were discouraged by a secret organisation about revealing the actual details.

Only a few people knew of the Stargate's existence, which included scientists and top government officials across Europe and the United States. The Anglo-Iraq war in 1941 was a British-led Allied military campaign against Rashid Ali, who seized power in Iraq in 1941, and later collaborated with Nazi Germany. During the 1930s, [*29] .Representatives of Nazi Germany and Fascist Italy attempted to gain favour with various Iraqi nationalists, as Nazi Germany went to Iraq to fight against the British, the undisclosed objective by the Nazis was to access to the Stargate.

The Nazis combed every ancient site in Europe and the Middle East, even going far as Tibet looking for ancient artifacts, which they believed had esoteric value that could be used within the Nazi's occult warfare division. Curiously enough, up until the expansion of the internet, the Anglo-Iraq war was seldom featured on TV documentaries or highlighted in print media. Since 2003, another Stargate was allegedly located in the basement of the former palace of Sadaam Hussein, presently within the heavily guarded Green Zone used by the U.S occupation authorities in central Baghdad. Academics generally regard the ancient Sumerian civilisation as the structural template for modern society.

For example, agriculture, artisan crafts and land management. Other technologies include medicine, writing (cuneiform) accounting, as the formation of writing that evolved was part of the process of monitoring commodities, usually administered by the higher classes, which included the "priests" as their role was to create records and inventories of wares.

Hence, the term "clerical" may be the root etymology relating to scribing documents especially by the spiritual leaders. The ancient Sumerians held a firm conviction of a "higher force," this prominent force is outlined in The Twelfth Planet that was published in 1976 by the author Zecharia Sitchin whose main project was to analyse Mesopotamian and Sumerian iconography and symbolism.

Illustration: Ziggurat of Ur, constructed in 2100 B.C.E. by the king Ur-Nammu of the Third Dynasty.

He highlighted that the Anunnaki came to earth 500,000 years ago from an undiscovered planet called Nibiru. According to ancient astronaut theorists, the Anunnaki reproduced with humans, eventually creating a race of human-alien hybrids, finally using the hybrid offspring as slaves to mine gold. Sitchin's views have been universally criticised by conventional academics as pseudo-history. Moreover, academics maintain that Sitchin purposely distorted the Sumerian texts by misusing the interpretations. However, this may be due to the method he implemented while interpreting the transcripts.

Moreover, his niece outlined that he did not write within an academic protocol, this being the prime reason why Sitchin's work was under criticism. Specialists in Sumerian languages could unpick his work by the means of standard academic criticism. He just went straight ahead and published his work without any academic feedback.

THE IRAQ STARGATE:

Researchers and authors have theorised that the device was a legacy from an advanced race of entities, possibly the Anunnaki. The device had the ability to generate a transferable wormhole or previously labelled as a one-dimensional tube and may have used the Einstein–Rosen Bridge principle.

A concept devised by Albert Einstein and physicist Nathan Rosen in 1935, a theoretical structure [a wormhole] that links to different points in spacetime, based on a singular explanation of the Einstein field equations. There is a network of related structures across Iraq and Iran, which according to researchers, may have the ability to create portals. One possible additional location of another Stargate could be within the Ziggurat of Ur; this site was also investigated by the U.S military. On previous surveys of the Ziggurat, the structure appeared to be composed of sun-baked bricks, which made up the central core of the edifice. The external facings would include fired bricks. Each step was slightly smaller than the step below it. The facings were glazed in different colours that may maintain an astrological significance. When Saddam came into power, he promptly gathered a team of his own scientists to restore and eventually activate the device.

Saddam knew that other countries would be monitoring his project, and emphasised, 'simply for the purpose of heritage', it was described as "Saddam Hussein's mission to rebuild Babylon."

George Bush senior was the former head of the CIA, the only organisation who knew about arcane scientific devices. This may be the case as George W Bush may have received this information from his father. It was often implied, the 9/11 bombings were a ruse to invade Iraq. One interpretation by author and researcher Elizabeth Vegh, believed the Stargate was disclosed in the Book of Revelation Chapter 9.

Vegh believed that "the pit of the abyss" described one of the portals being activated. However, as to date any technological theory on how the Stargate worked is still unknown.

Chapter 9 of the Book of Revelation:

"The fifth angel sounded, and I saw a star from the sky which had fallen to the earth. The key to the pit of the abyss was given to him.[*30]

Revelation 9:2

He opened the pit of the abyss, and smoke went up out of the pit, like the smoke from a {TR adds "great"} burning furnace. The sun and the air were darkened because of the smoke from the pit.

Revelation 9:3

Then out of the smoke came forth locusts on the earth, and power was given to them, as the scorpions of the earth have power.

Revelation 9:13

The sixth angel sounded. I heard a voice from the horns of the golden altar which is before God,

Revelation 9:14 Saying to the sixth angel who had one trumpet, "Free the four angels who are bound at the great river Euphrates!"

Revelation 9:15

The four angels were freed who had been prepared for that hour and day and month and year, so that they might kill one third of mankind.

Revelation 9:16

The number of the armies of the horsemen was two hundred million {literally, "ten thousands of ten thousands"}. I heard the number of them. *Quoted from World English Bible.*

According to researchers, other stargate's may be located across the Middle East; there has been an alleged report of a portal site in Afghanistan located on the outskirts of Sheberghan. No other recent features have been discovered to date regarding the Iraq Stargate, but the subject is still debated.

THE STRANGE CASE OF RUDOLPH FENTZ

Extract given with kind permission from Christopher Berry:

Over the years, there have been incidents of people who go missing or just vanish without a trace. In 1760 Shepton Mallet, Somerset, UK.

Owen Parfitt, a former sailor would sit on the front porch of his house during the summer months, wearing a heavy greatcoat often chatting to passers-by, telling them yarns about his adventures. One evening his sister and her young helper Susannah Snook found his coat propped against the front door. They thought he might be somewhere in the house. Hours later, both women went into the town looking for him. Being that Owen was riddled with arthritis he was also a huge man it would have been almost impossible for him to just wander off. The women asked the farm hands who worked in the fields close to the house, if they had seen him. They replied, 'No we haven't'. His sister continued to search the town thinking he may have moved, though having health problems, would be highly unlikely. This 200-year-old case has never been solved.

A similar incident happened in the late 19th century to a man from Coventry, Warwickshire England. He was a blacksmith by trade, and held the reputation of having superhuman strength. The blacksmith set a challenge stating that he could run 35 miles non-stop from Birmingham to Rugby. He set off by running along the main road, however about 25 miles later; he vanished, as described by onlookers "into thin air." His friends scoured the area in

an attempt to find how it happened. They found nothing, not even a piece of clothing. Some believe that when people disappear without a trace, may have slipped into a parallel dimension or even another timeline, as this may have been the case with Rudolph Fentz.

In 1950 around June 11:15 pm, a man wearing Victorian era clothes, looking startled and disoriented began to wander off onto the middle of a busy intersection in Times Square, New York City. Witnesses described how the man seemed to be wandering around in a state of panic. Within minutes, was knocked down, and killed by a passing taxi. The police arrived on the scene and began to look for identification.

They went through his pockets and found items that included $70 dollars' worth of obsolete banknotes, a 5¢ copper token from a saloon bar that no longer exists, a bill from a stable that was located on Lexington Avenue, for washing a carriage and feeding a horse. None of these items showed any sign of aging despite being near 100years old. The officers also found business cards with the name, 'Rudolph Fentz' along with a letter posted from Philadelphia postmarked 1876. Captain Hubert V. Rihm of the NYPD Missing Persons Department investigated and eventually tracked down Rudolph Fentz's daughter-in-law. She said that Fentz had disappeared in 1876 when he was twenty-nine years old. When Rihm checked missing person's records, he found an entry dated in 1876 for a 'Fentz'. The details on the report were an exact match for the unidentified man who had been knocked down and killed in Times Square. The story of Rudolph Fentz began to circulate throughout the European paranormal network since the early 1970s. Later in the mid 1990's the growth and accessibility of the internet, online magazines and forums propelled the story across the world.

The case of Rudolph Fentz has been reported more often as a reproduction of facts and presented as evidence for the existence of time travel. It was generally believed as a true story and a genuine mystery, which many people used to argue that inadvertent time travel could actually happen. In 2000, the story caught the attention of folklore researcher Chris Aubeck, who decided to investigate its history.

He traced the story back to the 1972 May/June issue of the Journal of Borderland Research, which investigated paranormal phenomena and UFO sightings; he also published the Rudolph Fentz story as a factual report. [*31] [*32]

One of the supporting factors of the article was the theory of 'holes between our dimension and the 4th dimension'. Aubeck wondered how *The Journal of Borderland Research* got hold of the story.

I'm Scared was originally published by Collier's magazine in September 1951. It was a story about an unnamed investigator, detailing his encounters with people who had time travel experiences in the New York area. One of the investigators interviewed Captain Hubert V. Rihm, who told him all about Rudolph Fentz.

In essence, The Journal of Borderland Research extracted something from a fictional short story and printed it as fact, while adding some theories triggering a popular mystery that was used to support the existence of time travel for more than thirty years. [*33]

The plot thickens, not everyone accepts that Jack Finney's I'm Scared is the true origin of the Rudolph Fentz urban legend. Numerous websites mention, as for example in 2007, a researcher working for the Berlin News Archive discovered something that throws doubt on the official story. I can't seem to trace who this person is or was, but apparently they found a newspaper article in the archives from April 1951.The article mentions Rudolph Fentz, his death in Times Square and his mysterious link to the person who went missing in 1876. Okay, so this newspaper article probably sourced the story from I'm Scared, too Right? Wrong. I'm Scared was published in Collier's in September 1951, five months after this article. It's an interesting twist that opens up a ton of possibilities.

Perhaps Rudolph Fentz really was a real person, but his inadvertent trip from 1876 to 1950 is an event that someone doesn't want us to know about. Perhaps the 'I'm Scared 'short story is part of an elaborate cover-up, a work of fiction disguising a real occurrence.

Why? to keep the truth about the existence of time travel a secret. It's now said that a number of researchers have found evidence of the real Rudolph Fentz, along with proof of his 1876 disappearance. Indeed, I found one website, Mystic Investigations, which cites unnamed sources inside the US government who have claimed that Rudolph Fentz's body was taken for study and is perfectly preserved in a top-secret lab. [*33]

PORTALS

The following examples include incidents, from individuals who may have stumbled into interdimensional portals and timeslips

The Green Door
Stoke on Trent: Staffordshire, UK
The following case originated from one of my contacts on a forum who was based in Staffordshire.

One morning, a young boy of seven decided to miss school and play truant, rather than face another beating from the brutal schoolmaster. It was now 9:00am, by now he would be ambling through the school gates, then into the classroom for registration. Instead, he was now wandering the streets, hiding behind walls, and avoiding people who might report him. He spotted an alleyway across the road called Old Hall Terrace, thinking 'won't be seen here'. As he continued along the track, he found himself behind a large wall situated behind a row of houses, an ideal spot to avoid people, who might inform the school board.

I could imagine the consequences for truancy in those days, especially in the early 1900s was serious. After walking a few yards, he came to a dead end in the form of a brick wall. While looking around, he noticed a small battered wooden, green door, which may have been a gate to a storage shed.

Out of curiosity, the boy went through the door crawling into the narrow gap, and found himself in an unusual location. This place had no comparison to the typical grimy industrial landscape of Hanley. He came across a path, which led to "an enormous garden."

The houses appeared different, in comparison to the soot-coated bricks that covered most of the local buildings, and the worn, weather-beaten front doors on his street. Warily, he continued along the path, and found himself in what could be a country village.

It appeared that most of the buildings were empty. As he continued walking, he noticed a large house and found that the front door was wide open. Inquisitively, he decided to walk inside the hallway. No one appeared to be in, so he walked up the stairs and saw a large room with a big window. The view from the upstairs window was unusual for the area, while viewing the unfamiliar landscape of trees and a river, he pondered 'All around here should be rows of houses "The boy began to feel strange and had the sudden urge to run from the house. He backtracked towards the entrance he came through and found himself back in the alleyway or local slang known as a ginnel. Two days later, he went back to the "ginnel" and scrambled through the small green door. This time, all he found were rubbish bins, no trees, or garden. *Eleven Years Later* At the outbreak of World War 1, the boy had grown up and was now serving his country as a soldier.

Based with the fourth Army Headquarters in France, that was part of the British Expeditionary Force. He was posted to the French village of Villiers Carbonnel, situated close to the river Somme.

In his free time, he decided to explore the nearby villages, one of them being a locale called Misery. Walking down the main street then turning off onto a track, he suddenly felt he had visited this place before, as it seemed incredibly familiar. Noticing the row of houses that were abandoned, he saw a large empty house, and decided to go inside. Most of the rooms were full of dead German soldiers.

He cautiously walked up the stairs and into a large bedroom, gripping his revolver, in case a German soldier was hiding in one of the alcoves. Moving towards the large but now broken window, he was shocked when he suddenly realised he had been here before. It was the same view through the window he experienced back in Hanley as a small boy, the same sloping valleys surrounded by trees, and a river.

PORTALS

The most curious thing, the house he was standing in, was located on a road called 'Rue Moulin' or 'Windmill Street'.

The boy who slipped into another location in the early 1900's was now a retired lecturer in mechanical engineering. In 1965, due to years of nagging curiosity, decided one day to visit the spot where he experienced his timeslip. He was standing in a place called Windmill St, then it clicked, he visited a location called Rue Moulin decades earlier which translated is Windmill Street. By now, most of the buildings were demolished or part of new building projects, he had an idea where the doorway may have been situated. However, the exact spot where the green door could have been was now part of a building site.

Timeslip Into The Future

Scholes, Kirklees, West Yorkshire, UK
Extract from Supernatural Pennines
By
Jenny Randles

The town of Holmfirth is located in the Kirklees district of West Yorkshire, England and situated close to the Pennines hills. Holmfirth was also famous for the BBC1 comedy sitcom called 'Last of the Summer Wine' which ran for 37 years from 1973-2010. Holmfirth is surrounded by villages, which include, Austonly, Arrunden, Burnlee, Brockholes, Fulstone, Jacksonbridge, Honley, Holme, Wooldale, and Scholes. Scholes village is about 1 mile (2 km) southeast and located above Holmfirth, and associated with a series of peculiar events witnessed by one of the residents, Audrey Hanson. Recalling as a small child around 1909 had a strange experience while playing in her house.

While she was playing, the whole of the room was suddenly filled with an intense glow that seemed to ooze from the walls as if 'painted in glow worms.' This left a magical atmosphere, which only subsided when the glow disappeared. During its presence, time seemed to stand still; there was a faint humming sound 'similar to a spinning top'. It was almost as if Audrey were 'plugged' into another dimension'.

Later on in her teens, Audrey had another strange experience, this was in 1915. While sitting on the banks of the local stream, she had a sudden feeling of mixed perceptions. The perspective of the place was more or less the same, the landscape and other features like the surrounding fields and woodland. However, something felt different, almost like being in another dimension. Audrey noticed a group of people walking along the footpath that ran adjacent to the wood; she recognised the group but did not know their names, as they were wearing clothes, which she thought 'were rather peculiar'.

PORTALS

[The material, length and shape especially the bright colours, this being 1915 would have been a strange site as most people , especially a small village in the north of England during this period , tended to wear almost puritanical attire of black and white and faded greys JPH]

As the group of people passed by, within a few seconds they vanished. Instinctively, Audrey got up to look and walked over to the footpath and looked down into the shaded entrance of the wood, nothing not a trace of activity, not even any footprints in the soil , they just disappeared into thin air.

Sixty Years later around the early 1970's Audrey went to the special place near the stream for a picnic. Unaware of sitting in the same spot on the bank as she did six decades ago, she noticed a group of people walking along the track. Feeling of 'I have seen this before?'

It was exactly the same group of people she saw years ago walking along the track, almost identical to that time. It was two of her neighbours and their friends wearing the exact same clothes and walking at the same pace, they did not disappear but carried on walking down the footpath towards the woods.

Manchester Time Slip
Courtesy of Jenny Randles from 'Supernatural Pennines'

In the winter of 1983, Derek Gibson from Cornwall was visiting north Manchester for a family wedding being unfamiliar with the area he went the day before to find the church prior to the ceremony. As he arrived at the location and saw the church, he was not terribly impressed describing it as dilapidated not only was it a dull overcast day he was looking at run down building, with rusty railings, very long grass, and what I took to be was a chapel with a square tower.

As he focused his gaze at the tower hoping he could reverse any disappointment and find any thread of quaintness. Moments later, glancing back at the church, it now looked completely different. The brickwork looked new, the stonework was clean and the iron railings coated in what appeared to be fresh black paint, the sky also was different, moving from overcast to a bright sunny day. "He could see figures wandering about near the church including a woman in her thirties wearing a long dress and holding a parasol with her hair clearly not in the modern style. Other people were also walking around the church quaintly dressed, even though they were talking, they were too far away for Derek to understand what was being said. Looking at them in bemusement, he saw the scene simply vanish only to return to what he had witnessed before, the rundown, unmanicured church on a typical grey Pennine winters day. About ten minutes later Derek experienced a similar "timeshift" when he saw a block of nearby modern shops suddenly change.

Now a series of wooden tables were in front with a group of poorly dressed men wearing grey flannels and flat caps sitting before what were much more Spartan looking than the shop fronts than had been there before. Again, the men were talking but their conversation was distant and muted, as he could not hear what they were saying.

Then, just as earlier, the scene evaporated in front of his eyes-to be replaced by modern shops and the surrounding streets, and the noise and the bustle of a busy road that passed directly in front.

Derek made several observations about these time slips. He described somehow witnessing this area as it was a century earlier. He said that the scene had flatness and dull colour, rather than the vividness of the modern world that it temporarily replaced. There was also a sense of "familiarity" to what he was seeing that he could not pin down. In addition, as the phenomenon was occurring he noted that all the ambient sounds were replaced by a feeling of detachment and "otherworldliness."

A possible explanation for Derek Gibson's experience could be comparative of a brief encounter in virtual reality...

'It seems improbable that Derek Gibson really visited the distant past and then returned home again on two successive occasions. More likely, this was essentially a phenomenon of consciousness-rather like the false awakenings, as he was seeing the past inside his mind as part of a waking dream and this was dubbed over the top of present reality to create a persuasive facsimile of the past in the form of a three dimensional running video' [*34].

The Bar That Never Was

The origins of the story are unknown, other accounts of this case happen in other locations across London.

While waiting for the Eurostar to Paris, two friends were looking forward to their first trip using the Channel Tunnel, as compared to previous excursions on the cross channel ferry.

Having booked a hotel not far from St Pancras station, they had four hours to spare before the journey.

Deciding to go for a wander, making sure they have enough time to return and collect their luggage from the hotel. They set off down the main road not far from St Pancras station. About fifteen minutes later, they noticed a side street that branched off from the main road. Out of curiosity, they continued to walk along the side street commenting on how the buildings looked so compressed. They notice a bar with an inactive red and blue neon sign "Casino" above the entrance, even from the outside; it had a kind of kitschy retro atmosphere, both agreeing it could be some sort of themed café bar. They entered the foyer, and noticed an extensive flight of stairs, which led to a small kiosk at the basement. A young woman who might be in her 20's with a 60's beehive hairstyle greeted them; then directed them to a corner table, taking their order. One thing that stood out was the presence of cigarette smoke. In this particular year, 2009 the smoking ban had been enforced for two years, as it was illegal to smoke in most public places, especially bars and clubs. It seemed ages since they ordered their drinks, they estimated it must have been about twenty minutes ago. They both got up and walked up to the bar attempting to prompt one of the staff by tapping on the counter.

No one responded while they stood there feeling puzzled by the situation, and decided to leave before they missed the train.

A few days later, when the friends returned from their trip, they decided to visit the Casino bar again, and traced their steps almost verbatim as they did previously.

They even asked passers-by and people in local shops 'Do you know of a 'Casino bar near here?' When they got back to the hotel, they asked the receptionist and a few of the older staff if they knew of any 'casino' bars, the answer was 'no sorry we don't'. In another attempt of retracing their steps, they eventually recognised the location where the bar would have been, however on that exact spot was now a newsagents.

Dunster House, Manchester Road, Rochdale, UK

Sometime ago, some former school friends and myself were discussing if they knew anyone who may have had any encounters relating to the paranormal. One of the group mentioned that one of his mates at college told him about an experience he had when he was about 7 years old. I managed to get some more information about the person and eventually arranged a meet at his house.

The man who wanted to remain anonymous will only use his initials, DM. Whether or not his encounter relates to some form of extensive haunting, or on deduction, D.M might have experienced a timeslip.

D.M is highly pragmatic, when I met him, he appeared to be a matter of fact no nonsense type of person. He does not have time for anything relating to the "paranormal, conspiracy theories etc."

To support his profile, he is a retired engineer and has a scientific approach to problem solving. D.M began his account, 'It was around spring 1967, at the time my house was located near Manchester Road, about 1.5 miles from Rochdale town centre. Close to my street were big Victorian houses that would have belonged to wealthy people such as mill owners and persons of high professional status. There was one building on Dunster Avenue, a large detached house; built in 1854. The architect was Joseph Clarke, who designed the house in the Gothic revival style. Later in 1863 Jonathan Nield, who was the managing partner of Fenton's Bank, installed additional features. D.M used to pass this house on a daily basis while walking to school, and was always curious if anyone actually lived there. 'It wasn't derelict, just empty; it was like that for years'.

Other people, who lived close by said, 'it has been in that state since the late 1950s.' D.M also wondered what was behind the huge wall that went all the way to the end of the street.

PORTALS

The main feature of the wall was a large wooden gate, which reminded him of an entrance to a castle.

One afternoon, D.M was passing the house while returning from school, and noticed the gate was open. Peering behind the gap, he discovered concealed behind the wall, the most impressive garden he ever saw.

Suddenly from around the corner, an old woman wearing a full-length black dress and wearing a distinctive bonnet...

The old woman looked at D.M with a curious expression then asked him 'Would you like to have a look?' slightly startled he replied 'yes'. He walked into the garden, which he described at the time as 'being really huge.' On reflection, D.M guessed that the style of the bonnet was from the mid-Victorian era, possibly the 1840s.

Describing what he saw 'The most imposing feature was the wisteria and weeping willow trees that encircled the fountain'.

'The sculpture in the centre of the fountain was of the Roman god Bacchius, the deity of agriculture, wine, and fertility'

I asked. 'How long did you stay there?' D.M replied, 'could have been an hour.' As D.M continued to explore the grounds, he noticed the old woman was now on the other side of the garden, walking through the door of a black wrought iron shed.

D.M wanted to catch her attention before he left, just to say thanks for allowing him to have a look around. He told me 'It was then; she just disappeared. I noticed the door was still open and looked inside, nothing- she just vanished.'

I asked. 'Was the iron shed merged so that you could walk into the house?' D.M replied. 'No it wasn't, it was detached and was built onto the edge of another wall on the opposite side where I stood'. 'There was no access point into the house whatsoever'.

'I waited for a while, but decided to set off back home'.

D.M told me another connected incident that happened a few years earlier at Dunster Avenue. In 1962, D.M's father (T.M) worked as a painter and decorator and was contracted to paint the interior of the house along with four of his workmates.

Even then, the place was still empty, and the job was going to take about two weeks to complete.

One afternoon, two of T.M's workmates were varnishing the large balustrade, when at the top of the landing, an old woman wearing a black dress and a bonnet stood looking at them. T.M asked, 'Is everything all right?' Suddenly she turned around and went up another flight of stairs to the upper level, T.M then shouted 'Careful the paint is still wet' he also noticed the woman went inside one of the rooms, while carrying a bundle of sticks on her back. Thinking that the woman might be deaf, T.M and one of his co-workers wanted to make sure the woman was not exposed to the wet paint on the bannister and stairs. Two of the men walked into the room, it was empty, one of the men said 'I bet she might have gone in there' pointing to a large walkthrough wardrobe. They looked inside…nothing 'probably a secret passage,' said T.M. The other men shouted around the house and checked all of the rooms. I asked D.M, do you think the woman was a ghost?

'No my dad said she had the composition like any other living person'.

About 2010, D.M and his father were discussing local history and the topic of conversation gradually led to discussing Dunster House.

D.M said 'the house had fantastic gardens' T.M replied 'when? You were too young'.

D.M maintained on what he saw was real 'I went in the back garden, it was 1967, there were wisteria vines, and a magnificent fountain'.

'No way', T.M replied. Still insistent D.M 'I did, it seemed well kept'.

T.M concluded... 'That's impossible, in the early to mid-1950s, me and your uncle, when we were about 10 years old, used to climb over the wall and play in what would have been a garden but this was full of weeds, and that fountain you mentioned was a pile of rubble !'.

I asked do you think somebody tidied the garden a couple of weeks earlier before you went in?'

D.M replied, 'No chance' I cannot understand how, I passed there every day, including the weekend. 'I did not see or hear anybody working on the garden'. Was this a time slip or a slide into another alternative dimension?

co-existing with that particular timeline in 1967? Dunster House was later demolished in November 1968.

Loch Ness Timeslip

In 2008, it has been reported that residents in the nearby towns close to Loch Ness are being woken up at night by a strange, low-frequency humming noise. The same phenomenon has been reported in other areas of the US and the UK, primarily in Taos, New Mexico, and remains unexplainable to this day.

'The Taos Hum affects 2% of the local population; the sound is similar to an idling or rumbling diesel engine; the frequency is around 20-40 hertz. This constant noise has been known to drive people mad. Some researchers have theorised that the hum is the result of unusual sensitivity of some people to electromagnetic noise created by the growing number of gadgets. 'Others say it's something to do with aliens or secret military experiments. Another theory claims it is the sound of the universe expanding. Blogger Sarah Hapgood reports on one visit to Loch Ness, she saw all the birdlife in the area going completely berserk around midnight – like something out of Alfred Hitchcock's *The Birds*. Could this be linked to the Taos Hum in some way? Are the birds sensitive to it as well?' [*35]

The Time Travelling Couple

Cited by author Andrew Collins in his book Alien Energy: In the mid-18th century a couple were travelling in a horse and trap near
Lochend on the northern shore of Loch Ness, they asked locals for the nearest inn. They met a local man who gave them directions to the nearest hostelry. With it being a small and remote place, the locals took interest in the couple's presence as they were from one of the larger towns in Scotland.

Later, the villagers were curious if the travellers arrived at the inn. The innkeeper could not explain what happened to the couple.

Local people speculated they might have been kidnapped or attacked by outlaws and thrown into the loch. A hundred years later in the mid-19th century, a man, and a woman walked into a local alms-house asking to seek refuge from the ongoing storm. The priest who took them in noted that they were wearing old-fashioned clothing and appeared to be very confused, unable to explain where they'd come from or how they had arrived in the area. [*36] Two days later, they disappeared 'Was it the same couple? Did the man and woman who disappeared in the mid-18th century slip go forward in time to the 19th? Did they slip back again after the two days – or to another time entirely?' [*36] As these strange cases occurred near Loch Ness, this invites the question, is there some form of portal within the region? Could the Loch Ness monster be a prehistoric entity that transfers back and forth through a time tunnel?

Earliest sightings go back to the 6th century by the Irish monk Saint Columba, who gave last rites to a man, who was drowned by a large water beast.' [*37] The most prevalent idea that could link geology and reports of paranormal activity is the Tectonic Strain Theory. I was inspecting the BGS geology map; I noticed three prominent fault lines that converge into the central section of Loch Ness.

The significance of geological fault lines relating to the Tectonic Strain Theory is that under certain conditions, disturbances in the fault lines can create localised electromagnetic activity, especially if the geological profile contains quartz crystals. When a geological shift occurs, especially when you have high levels of motion, this may be able to generate piezoelectricity. Moreover, this may develop into some form of hidden energy vortex or portal as similar examples have occurred in other locations.

Could the fault lines be part of the curious incidents related to the couple from the 18th century and the intermittent sightings of "Nessie," along with the low frequency noise? On the 18th September 1901, there was an earthquake graded on the $M=5$ Richter scale that was linked to the disturbance of the Great Glen Fault- one of the major fault lines that runs across Loch Ness.

It has been noted that prior to earthquakes most often, some people can hear low frequency sounds, described as a constant low rumbling as this is attributed to possible low frequency oscillation created by geological activity. These waves are reflected from the surface and "bounce off" generating a varied refraction of frequencies.

The outcome is the transmission of ultra-low frequencies or infrasound. In relation and to compare a similar case regarding the Hope Street timeslips, one researcher when studying the Hope Street cases, highlighted that infrasound may affect the temporal section of the brain creating altered perceptions.

ARE THERE ANY OTHER THEORIES BEHIND TIME SLIPS?

In the past, time travel and parallel universes by default have always been associated with science fiction. However, in recent decades, scientists have conducted experiments and mathematical theories, which led to the notion that there might be multiverses or even other dimensions that may coexist with our own. The primary view of modern physicists is that time is fluid; highlighting the interpretation, that space-time is a dynamic entity that responds to the presence of matter around it, or that space-time could be flexible and respond to substance within its environment as all matter travels through time. Every single subatomic particle has a single location in space, velocity, and possibly other parameters for every moment in time.

Time travel theories other perspectives:

Though being a vigilant physicist, Richard Feynman [1918-1988] once stated, 'There are other types of energy that we know nothing about, if they exist this may explain so called paranormal phenomena'.

The answer may lie in the study and recent discoveries in quantum mechanics. Research in this field include the "many-worlds interpretation" or (MWI); 'there are many worlds that exist in parallel, and within the same space and time as our own' [*38]

A variation of Hugh Everett's many-worlds interpretation (MWI) of quantum mechanics provides a resolution to the grandfather paradox that involves the time traveller arriving in a different universe instead of the actual location of origin they came from. It has been argued that since the traveller(s) arrive in a different universe's history and not their own history, this is not "genuine" time travel. [*39] Could this relate to timeslip cases when an individual has gone back or forward momentarily to a duplicate timeframe, but in a "different universe"?

Carl Sagan once suggested the possibility that time travellers could be here but are disguising their existence or are not recognized as time travellers. [*40] Some versions of general relativity suggest that time travel might only be possible within the region of spacetime…

that is warped in a certain way, and hence time travellers would not be able to travel back to earlier regions in spacetime, before this region existed. Stephen Hawking stated that this would explain why the world has not already been overrun by "tourists from the future."[*41] Several experiments have been carried out to try to entice future humans, who might have invented time travel technology, to come back and demonstrate it to people of the present time. Events such as Perth's Destination Day or MIT's Time Traveller Convention heavily publicized permanent advertisements of a meeting time and place for future time travellers to meet. [*42]

In 1982, a group in Baltimore, Maryland, identifying itself as the Krononauts, hosted an event of this type welcoming visitors from the future.[*43] These experiments only stood the possibility of generating a positive result demonstrating the existence of time travel, but have failed . So far—no time travellers are known to have attended either event. Some versions of the many-worlds interpretation have created the suggestion that future humans have travelled back in time, but have travelled back to a certain time and place, but in a parallel universe. [*44]

ARE THERE ANY OTHER THEORIES BEHIND TIME SLIPS?

It was the Austrian physicist Erwin Schrödinger, who in 1935 provided a thought experiment while at a conference in Copenhagen. He also credited Einstein, Podolsk, and Rosen as the contributors. The basic premise is that subatomic particles have a dual nature, as they can be in two places at once. He demonstrated this by using a hypothetical model, known as *Schrödinger's Cat*. 'Schrödinger stated that if you place a cat and a device that could kill the cat (a radioactive atom) in a box and seal it. You would not know if the cat was dead or alive until you opened the box, so that until the box was opened, the cat was (in a sense) both dead and alive.' [*45].

According to one article in The New York Times -May 8th 2019, scientists at IBM used a quantum computer to time reverse a Qubit (a manufactured
particle of information) back to 1/1,000,000th of a second. Similar examples of time manipulation have been active using photons as one of the key elements that have been used in research, for example in Russia, Japan, and Australia, by applying a variety of experiments. However, it will be sometime before we witness anything on a larger scale.

Generally, people in most cultures perceive the world in three-dimensions, this inherent awareness keeps us grounded in reality. The concept of a fourth dimension of time is at present a speculative notion and would not register mechanically or consciously.

Three-dimensional concepts are length, width, height; also, the collective perception is that the flow of time is sequential.

Current research within the realms of quantum fields may eventually hold more significance, as compared to the Newtonian standpoint; moreover, Newton would not have been aware of the existence of subatomic particles.

Newton believed that absolute time was physically undetectable and could only be understood mathematically.

The on-going experiments with the Large Hadron Collider at the CERN institute have opened the doors to new concepts in physics. In 2012, the discoveries of the Higgs boson particle, which according to physicists at the Vanderbilt University speculate that the Higgs singlet may be able to traverse through space/ time.

One article from a science journal implied that the Higgs singlet [*singlet state usually refers to a system in which all electrons are paired*] [*46] Once developed, the particle may be able to travel into other dimensions, in the form of data but not for actual human time travel. Other perspectives include the block universe theory, 'The universe is a giant block of all the things that ever happen at any time and at any place' [*47]. On interpretation, the past, present and future all exist — and are equally real [*48].

In addition, the varied interpretations by Einstein, Feynman, and Hawking all propose that the past, present, and future all exist simultaneously.

There have been collected examples of on-going time distortion experiments carried out by scientists, who used Nikola Tesla's research notes on high potential and high frequency electrical magnetism.

Nikola Tesla (1856-1943) was a Serbian-American inventor who also created ground-breaking inventions within the areas of electrical and mechanical engineering. One of his key attributes was the design of the alternating current (AC) electricity supply system; he also experimented with wireless energy. While developing additional methods with the wireless energy transmission experiment, as part of the process he came across scalar or longitudinal waves. Scalar waves are formed when two electromagnetic emissions of the same frequency are exactly out of phase (opposite to each other) and the amplitudes subtract and cancel or terminate each other.

One of the methods used for generating scalar waves is to bind electrical wires in the form of a Möbius coil, which consists of strands of wires, formed in the shape of a figure eight; this principle can apply to any size. As electric current flows through the wires in opposite directions, the opposing electromagnetic fields from the two wires cancel each other out: the outcome is a scalar wave. It is claimed that scalar waves may have the ability to travel faster than light and capable of passing through solid objects unlike conventional radio waves that can be impeded by certain materials like lead, concrete blocks, aluminium.

Scalar waves may have the capability to traverse into other dimensions. The abilities of scalar waves are considered to be beyond the realms of conventional physics and still under discussion.

Further studies from a diverse range of academics have created a compilation of possible explanations as for instance "quantum entanglement".

One example, a specific location that retained some form of energy or "presence" at a precise moment in 1900, and at that specific point, was to merge or entangle with energy from the year 2000. Merging with the electromagnetic waves [EM], and possibly interacting with the subatomic realm of single photons, which in the process of interaction, may manifest on a larger scale, as a timeslip projection?

It was around 80 years ago when scientists discovered that a single photon [particle of light,] could be at two locations at the same time. Recently, according to the journal Nature Physics, (23) a team of international scientists succeeded in creating a molecule composed of 2,000 atoms to occupy two locations at the same time. Which invites the idea, what if this could happen on an even larger scale? If unexpectedly the other location or possible other dimension could be received for a brief moment?

X Points

Back in the 1990's- NASA's Polar spacecraft, spent years studying the Earth's magnetosphere. While continuing to review and analyse the data, the NASA scientists' uncovered locations that had anomalies containing 'electron diffusions' which are caused by the sudden joining of magnetic fields that are able to push streams of charged particles called X points. Xpoints occur when the Earth's magnetic field is connected by the solar wind from the Sun, which contributes to the polar magnetic storms. The magnetic fields on Earth somehow form a connection with the solar wind motion, which creates a portal. The magnetosphere extends outwards approximately 65,000 kilometres or 40.000 miles above the surface of the earth. Observations by the Themis spacecraft launched by NASA and with the collaboration from the European Space Administration (ESA) who provided the cluster probes, suggest that these portals are active at random intervals by opening and closing a dozen of times a day. These anomalies can also vary in size, and fluctuate in activity; some may appear for a matter of minutes or can be active for days. These particles flow through the openings, which create the heating of the Earth's upper atmosphere and activate geomagnetic storms.

In addition, others speculate about the potential of these magnetically charged particles, as the activity pending on the magnitude of the flux and the location were able to generate portals. NASA launched the Multi scale Mission (MMS) project in 2015 the aim was to find what is contained within the portals. This has fired up rumours on a variety of forums, as one web site claimed that NASA admitted that the notions of Earth portals could exist. This prompted an opinion, if there was an opening that was linked to an X point located on Earth, could being in one of these "points" at a particular time, create the experience of slipping into another dimension?

ARE THERE ANY OTHER THEORIES BEHIND TIME SLIPS?

What about earth bound or localised time travel?

A brief description often used, is "a tear in the fabric of time" or a fissure, a ripple in the timeline. Some buildings and locations may have triggers within their structure or environment that react to certain conditions: for example, the time of year [seasonal], weather, electromagnetic environmental frequencies, environmental alignments and building materials. People who have experienced a time slip describe altered vision, bright lights, or oblique angled light shades. For example, a bright sunny day suddenly alters into abnormal sudden darkness.

Other accounts include unusual sound transference, feeling of detachment. In addition, highly sensitive people can sense approaching earthquakes and thunderstorms; the most common description is a tingling sensation, headaches, ringing in the ears, moreover, could similar types of individuals who are prone to hyper perception, experience a traversal into another dimension or timeline? For example, a woman in her mid-30s was walking near the city walls in York, UK. As she glanced towards the main gate, a burst of intense sunlight obscured her vision, as she tried to adjust her eyesight from the bright glare, seeing people passing by dressed in medieval clothes, also the whole street was covered in straw, then two wooden carts trundled past.

The woman emphasised it was not a historical re-enactment or themed exhibition for a museum showcase. Within a space of roughly three minutes, everything was back to normal.

Vortexes and Portals

Depending on a person's perspective, portals are defined as points of entry to other dimensions, usually believed to be spiritual or ethereal gateways. Vortexes can be found in places that have potential concentrations of variable gravitational forces, which in some cases can bend light and affect the human energy field; these anomalies can be located at various locations on Earth.

Furthermore, a portal has been described as having weak membranes within the local energy fields, which surround other dimensions. There is a link between vortexes and portals as for example, whether or not the Brighton case may be down to hallucinations. However, if two witnesses at varied times describe a swirling light appearing from the end wall of a house, or a strange spinning light appearing in the middle of the road could there be some form of anomaly within that proximity ? It is believed that the most prominent ancient sites are located on portals as for example ; Puerta de Hayu Marca in Peru otherwise known as the 'Gateway to the Gods' also Abu Ghurab, Egypt, The Place of The Gods, Stonehenge, Wiltshire, UK. The Sumerian Stargate is close to the ancient Mesopotamian city of Eridu, and Gobekli Tepe, Turkey, Sedona, Arizona U.S known as the "Doorway of the Gods" associated with strange sounds emanating from the rocks. In the 1800's near Sedona, a Native American tribal elder described how three tribesmen came across a glowing archway.

ARE THERE ANY OTHER THEORIES BEHIND TIME SLIPS?

The archway could have been activated, possibly by the electromagnetic properties emanating from the nearby rocks, creating an effect on the visitor's psyche in the form of hallucinations in this case an "archway."

In May 2015, a photographer based in Holland set up his camera pointing towards the sky taking images of cloud formations. Instead, he managed to capture the formation of what appeared to be a mid-air portal; the anomaly appeared above the town of Groningen located northeast of the Netherlands.

Some have suggested this may have been linked to a simultaneous experiment conducted with the Large Hadron Collider, in Switzerland. According to a posting on the CERN website, an experiment conducted on the 2oth May 2015 using the method of proton collision, produced a "record breaking" 13 TeV [Tera-electron volts]

Dowsing:

Dowsing is described as a method of divination that has been used for centuries. Dowsers search for hidden water sources, metal ores, and oil without the use of scientific apparatus, even during the Vietnam War U.S troops used dowsing rods to locate hidden tunnels. The types of equipment include; L or Y shaped divining rods. These are made of wood or metal as an example, modified old coat hangers. Pendulums are also used and vary in shape and size; these are usually brass, or crystal. While dowsers in most situations are able to detect geological anomalies, e.g. fault lines, moreover, in Germany, Switzerland, and the Netherlands, dowsing is a respected skill often employed by some construction companies, for locating potential geopathic stress zones and "cancer" lines.

While searching for concealed resources a dowser will either ask verbally or think on their intended target source. They will verify a pattern, by watching the rods move either clock- wise or counter – clockwise, either direction is subjective.

I met two dowsers from North Wales who claimed they were able to detect the presence of buildings even though the structures no longer existed. The dowser and his group were able to detect walls and other related structures. While using their dowsing rods, two of the group members felt a presence of an outline as they let the rods trace the shape of the hidden dimensions. The results of the residual proportions were, 16ft in length [4.8 meters] by 10ft [3.048 meters] wide. This generated the idea, what if under certain conditions, these structures briefly rematerialize, as similar to the *Rougham Mystery* case. The dowsers conducted a count by 'asking' the rods to turn counter-clockwise, as each turn would represent a century in reverse, the rods stopped on seven and a half turns. On research, two of the dowsers examined the maps and land records of that particular site.

The result of their field research uncovered, the particular section they focused on was part of a building that dated to the 12th century.

On conclusion, the dowsers referred to this presence as a possible ethereal trace. Moreover, the possible building materials used in that period would have been wood, or wattle and daub, which more than likely would have disintegrated over time leaving no visual residue. One of the dowsers commented 'this experiment could explain when people sometimes feel they have slipped back in time, and perhaps the presence of places or structures may virtually re-emerge at certain intervals, having similar components of a hologram.

Natural Networks

Alternative researchers of geological anomalies believe there is a network of geophysical lines that span the globe often referred to as the "Crystalline Grid," and defined of being part of the higher multidimensional vibrational network. The existence of the grid invites contentious opinions as most part of the viewpoint covers spirituality and new age pseudoscience. However, some attributes may have some persuasive aspects that may link to hidden geological related frequencies or a common reference known as energy lines that traverse across the globe. The grid passes through well-known ancient sites Machu Picchu in Peru, The Pyramids of Giza in Egypt, Stonehenge in the UK; this will include secondary sites, such as churches, standing stones and stone circles. If anyone happened to find themselves inside an intersection point within the Crystalline Grid network, and the crossing generated certain frequencies, this might create a concealed vortex, which may alter a person's perception or the sense of being within another dimension?

Vortex hunters

One of the key indicators vortex hunters look for are the unknown types of energy found amongst limestone and quartz deposits. Moreover, other dimensional fluxes located within the convergence of earth fault lines, underground streams that generate minor electrical charges, which can potentially create a vortex. If you happen to locate one, how would you know? You would experience a tingling sensation, dizziness, and dislocation or when an individual feels they have slipped into another place.

Vortex researchers use EMF meters, and a standard radio tuned in to the FM frequency. If you are within the centre of what you believe is the location of a natural magnetic vortex you find the radio signal fades out completely. Other indications researchers observe are bald patches on grass or if you plant a tree within a vortex, most plants and trees tend to grow distorted.

Sound Frequencies

There are other factors as for example certain rocks and mineral veins amplify naturally occurring sound frequencies. For example, infra or low frequency sound, has been described 'the sort of noise you can feel', generally occurring before seismic activity, even in the UK there are the occasional earthquakes.

The frequency is located within the electromagnetic spectrum range between 3 to 30 Hz. In addition, underground watercourses, drainage pipes, and deep tunnels generate low frequency vibrations. These sound emissions can alter a person's perception as the constant pulsation from the infrasound frequency ranges from 1 Hz to 20 Hz, can also affect the temporal lobes of the brain, which creates a dreamlike state. Most long distance lorry drivers experience this by describing a constant "hum" from the engine, which can generate a hypnotic mind condition.

ARE THERE ANY OTHER THEORIES BEHIND TIME SLIPS?

Researchers claim the frequency was within the range of 6HZ. Certain locations could be situated on sections that transmit these frequencies either natural or manufactured. Moreover, the ELF occurrences could initiate an individual to experience the feeling of being detached or the sensation of entering another dimension.

One possible cause that could trigger a time slip experience might be activated by locations that have experienced conflict, prime example large battle sites. To invite the question, would the constant use of high explosives, both aerial and land-based bombs hitting certain points in the landscape produce the potential energy created by the constant explosions? The sonic and physical outputs of bomb strikes and intense explosions could potentially create a "tear" within unknown or hidden portal locations. As for example, cases in the book outline events that relate to the Second World War. Perhaps the ordnance technology in WW2 was more potent than the previous conflicts and combined with the intense human emotions, may trigger a potential "tear" and activate a glitch. As for example, constant bombing culminating from the London blitz may have activated the Waterloo Station incident and the East End Bombsite: Napoleonic Timeslip may have reanimated entities, who at the time were part of a previous crucial conflict in British history?

The Mandela Effect

The term originated in 2010 by a self-styled paranormal consultant called Fiona Broome in reference to her own false memory of the death of South African leader Nelson Mandela thinking that he died in prison in the 1980's, when in fact Nelson Mandela died in 2013.

Examples of these mistaken references have been distributed by a multitude of people across the world. Others claim that part of the Mandela Effect could relate to a possible occurrence of a time glitch or an interdimensional shift. Just to outline other examples of the Mandela Effect include Henry VIII's [1491 to 1547] portrait with a turkey leg in his hand many people are convinced they have seen the image in history books. Some dispute the "turkey question" highlighting that that turkeys being a native of North America were not available during his reign, however, the turkey was introduced by William Strickland in 1526, but only a small number of the birds that he had were sold near Bristol docks, and wouldn't have been available for widespread distribution at that time. Other examples listed include the Monopoly Man with monocle vs. without monocle, Rock group "Queen" song ending with "We are the champions" vs. "of the world." Some are plainly misinterpretations, which relate to spelling and pronunciation of places, books, and TV series. One prime and common example is when you are convinced when a celebrity, actor, musicians etc., who you think may be alive or have passed away or vice versa. The possible factor is the escalation of media outlets over the last 20 years. This has created a global overload of information being sent through TV channels, magazines, and websites. The outcome of this overload may create fragmented actualities, triggered by the multiple variations of a story or feature, as these variables can modify the change in perception.

ARE THERE ANY OTHER THEORIES BEHIND TIME SLIPS?

For example, some audiences will misread an article and overlook the key points, and create their own brief conclusions on what they believed were the informative points of a

feature. Another related factor to false memory is déjà vu, which is …"I am sure I have seen this before?" Some individuals are also convinced there is a "leakage" from a parallel or a mirror dimension, which briefly replaces our own for a few moments.

Déja vu is the result of a short-term memory feature being unconsciously sent to the long-term memory section of your brain.

It is the Large Hadron Collider, which the conspiracy theorists tend to focus on believing the LHC is the source of strange peculiar events and may be behind generating interdimensional slips.

One of the core aims is to shed light on the esoteric world of particle physics. The conspiracy sector believes that the entire on-going experiments, the secret projects, are behind universal particle manipulation, and have rebranded the experiments as "The Cern Mandela Effect." They also claim that the scientists at CERN are unaware of taking potential risks with the newly discovered elements (atomic and subatomic particles) as these may create minor "black holes" , the idea of black holes being generated by the LHC was often debated years before its launch on the 10th September 2008 . In January 2016, an American tourist filmed a vortex being formed above the city of Geneva. This incident fuelled the belief that the LHC could alter time by distorting the earth's magnetic field, and the possibility of contributing to changing variables in perception by globally altering quantum particles, even creating a scatter of mini portals. Conclusion, déjà vu may be linked to accessing previous genetic memory, as the mind may inherit a time, or place, from a previous ancestor, either paternal or maternal.

Perhaps the inherited memories could materialise in a person's subconscious mind into imagining they have "slipped" into another place. As regarding the Mandela Effect, some believe that they have transferred into another mirror dimension, as this may be a type of third dimensional *pareidolia** or plainly speaking another possible case of false memory intrusion and altered perception.

* pareidolia: the tendency for incorrect perception of a stimulus as an object, pattern or meaning known to the observer, such as seeing shapes in clouds, seeing faces in inanimate objects or abstract patterns, or hearing hidden messages in music [wikipedia.org/wiki/Pareidolia]

THE ROUGHAM MYSTERY
By
Carl Grove

Introduction

For one hundred and fifty years, the small Suffolk village of Rougham, lying four miles south-east of Bury St. Edmunds, has been the site of a curious phenomenon. Many people have reported seeing houses in places where no houses exist, and these buildings have subsequently disappeared. Most people with an interest in the unexplained a term that I prefer to others such as "paranormal" -- will be aware of this phenomenon, but usually only in the context of one particular case, the Wynne-Allington report, which dates from 1926. This case was one of the first of its type to be featured in a radio broadcast and a subsequent book, and the casual enquirer might be forgiven for considering it an isolated incident. It is not, and it needs to be considered in the context of at least 20 such cases reported not only in Rougham, but in a wider area in and around Bury st Edmonds. Such cases are now generally referred to as time slips,

implying that the witnesses have in some sense gained access to a past period. For many years the most famous, such event known to most people was the Versailles case, which dates from 1901. Two English academic ladies visiting Paris apparently found themselves wandering the gardens of the famous palace in the time of Marie Antoinette, and later spent much time researching old documents and maps, subsequently publishing their findings in a remarkable book, entitled An Adventure. [*1]

Considerable controversy around their claims has continued to the present day, and it is fair to say that no conventional explanation can be found that convincingly accounts for their experience.

However, a more careful analysis of historical records casts doubt upon the authors' own conclusions regarding the specific period that they visited. I have been interested in the Rougham phenomena for several years, and particularly so because my wife used to live there, and had a couple of similar experiences herself. On one occasion, while travelling in to work on a scooter, she saw men pushing a broken-down car a short distance ahead of her. They briefly went out of sight around a slight turn and when she reached it seconds later, there was no sign of men or cars. Later she had another experience in the same place, this time involving an elderly lady cyclist.

About Rougham

The village of Rougham lies a few miles to the south-east of Bury St Edmunds in Suffolk. Historically, it is probably typical of many East Anglian villages. There is much evidence of Roman activity and settlement, including the recent discovery of the burial site of a prominent Roman personage. The village church is a massive structure, suggesting that at one time the village was larger and wealthier, perhaps, than it later became. In common with other communities, the people resented the financial and other demands of the powerful Bury St Edmunds Abbey, and after they refused to pay the Abbey's taxes monks took retribution by burning their houses to the ground, later using a clever piece of disinformation to claim that the attack was actually in response to an outbreak of plague. Satellite imagery on Google maps clearly shows the streets and buildings as ghostly images around the church.

Resettlement took place further south and the nucleus of the village was then the north end of Kingshall Street, now the main road between Rougham and the nearby Bradfield St. George. Rougham airfield, lying to the north-west, played a major role in WWII, and afterwards mounted regular air shows and other events.

The airfield is haunted, and the Tower Association is active in studying the phenomena. Not too much should be read into this activity: most English towns and villages have hauntings of various kinds and degrees.

However, later on we will see that Rougham perhaps has a greater variety of unusual phenomena than other places. The geology of the area is dominated by glacial deposition: this could be important in finding causal factors with regard to the alleged time slips. Obviously, a glacier could pick up any and all types of rock on its journey south.

Regarding the geology of the area, while comparing the geological map, there are no geological fault lines, which are associated with strange activity such as hauntings and time slips. In recent years, Bury St Edmonds has begun to encroach on the village, and the construction of the Moreton Hall estate led to the demolition of several old houses that were originally considered to be part of Rougham. New estates have been built in the north of the village and there has been sporadic building along Kingshall Street. The largest landholder is Rougham Estates, which has been managed by the Agnew family since 1904. Google Earth has imagery for all of Kingshall Street and part of the road going on to Bradfield St. George. Google Maps also provides satellite photos of the entire area.

THE WYNNE-ALLINGTON CASE

Early in 1926, a new rector and his family took up residence at Rougham Rectory. The Rev. Arthur Wynne was born in West Derbyshire in 1871. He seems to have married in Glossop in 1900, but I have been unable to trace details of his wife. His daughter Ruth was born, also in West Derbyshire, in 1908. Ruth was a teacher; perhaps today we would call her a tutor, as she seems to have had only one pupil, a girl called Evelyn Allington, born in Mutford, near Beccles, in 1912. By October 1926, a pattern had developed Evelyn's lessons took place in the mornings, and in the afternoons, the two young ladies took long walks to familiarise themselves with the area. Thus it was that one autumn afternoon, they made the fateful decision to walk to the church at Bradfield St George. Leaving the churchyard, they headed south along a footpath which was pointing in roughly the right direction.

Ruth Wynne later stated [2]: One dull, damp afternoon, I think in October '26, we walked off through the fields to look at the church of the neighbouring village, Bradfield St. George. In order to reach the church, which we could see plainly ahead of us to the right, we had to pass through a farm-yard, whence we came out onto a road. We had never previously taken this particular walk, nor did we know anything about the topography of the hamlet of Bradfield St. George. Exactly opposite us on the further side of the road and flanking it, we saw a high wall of greenish-yellow bricks. The road ran past us for a few yards, then curved away from us to the left. We walked along the road, following the brick wall round the bend, where we came upon tall, wrought-iron gates set in the wall. I think the gates were shut or one side may have been open.

The wall continued on from the gates and disappeared round the curve of the road. Behind the wall and towering above it was a cluster of tall trees. From the gates, a drive led away among these trees to what was evidently a large house.

We could just see a corner of the roof above a stucco front in which I remember noticing some windows of Georgian design. The rest of the house was hidden by the branches of the trees. We stood by the gates for a moment, speculating as to whom lived in this large house, and I was rather surprised that I had not already heard of the owner amongst the many people who had called on my mother since our arrival in the district. This house was one of the nearest large residences to our own, and it seemed odd that the occupants had not called.

However, we then turned off the road along a foot-path leading away to the right of the church which was perhaps under a hundred yards off. On leaving the church, we cut down through the church yard into the fields and home, without returning to the road or to the farm-yard. It was then drizzling rain. On arriving home, we discussed the big house and it's possible occupants with my parents, and then thought no more of it. My pupil and I did not take the same walk again until the following spring. It was, as far as I can remember, a dull afternoon with good visibility in February or March. We walked up through the farm-yard as before, and out onto the road. when, suddenly, we both stopped dead of one accord and gasped. 'Where's the wall?' we queried simultaneously. It was not there. The road was flanked by nothing but a ditch, and beyond the ditch lay a wilderness of tumbled earth, weeds, mounds, all overgrown with the trees which we had seen on our first visit. We followed the road round the bend, but there were no gates, no drive, no corner of a house to be seen. We were both very puzzled. At first, we thought that our house and wall had been pulled down since our last visit. But on closer inspection it showed a pond and other small pools amongst the mound where the house had been visible. It was obvious that they had been there a long time. [2. Bennett, E. Apparitions and Haunted Houses]

No one they asked seemed to know anything about the house. Miss Wynne sent her account of the mystery house to Sir Ernest Bennett, who was presenting a programme on supernatural topics on BBC radio. He managed to locate Evelyn Allington, who confirmed her teacher's story.

However, neither witness was able to explain exactly where they had seen the house, although they apparently became familiar with the area over the next four years, and often returned to that spot. A local historian and psychic researcher, Mr. Leonard Aves., revisited the case in the 1970's.

A man with extensive local knowledge, he began his investigations as a total sceptic. However, far from disproving anything, he ended up finding more evidence to back up Miss Wynne's story. He was unable to find anything, which could have caused the witnesses to believe that a house was visible. When interviewed in the Bury Free Press in 1978, he discounted the theory that they may have seen a mirage. *The possible route, which the two witnesses walked, is shown by dashes. At the end of the ditch, a gap in the hedge may represent the position where the iron gates may have been.*

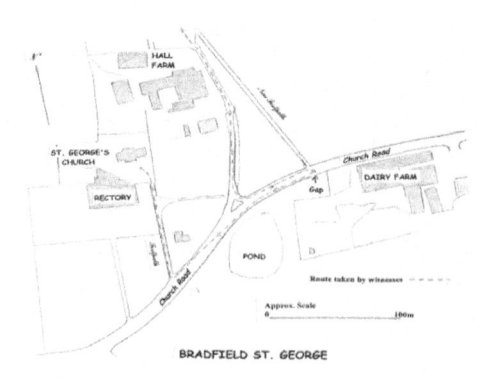

Illustration by Carl Grove

THE JAMES COBBOLD ARTICLE

In 1975, the gardening magazine Amateur Gardening published a short article [6] that dealt with the mystery house of Rougham.
Its author, James Cobbold, was a local resident
with an interesting tale to tell. Not only he, but also his great-grandfather, had allegedly seen the house. According to Cobbold (a pen-name), he had first heard about the vanishing house in 1911-12 from a girl who would have been approximately his own age, 11 or 12. He had scoffed at her claims, which suggest, of course, that sightings of the house must have been fairly common at that time. However, later, discussing it with his grandmother, he discovered that her own father had seen it in around 1860. Robert Palfrey had been making a haystack on a warm June evening when he glanced over to see that a house had suddenly appeared on the other side of the lane (later Cobbold would locate it in the vicinity of Colville's Grove. It was of red brick, and set in a garden with flowerbeds full of blooms, edged with red bricks placed slantwise. It had two wrought iron gates, one 4 ft. wide, the other 9-10 ft.

A sudden chill had developed. Palfrey went home (he lived, Phil Sage thinks, at the northern end of Kingshall Street) and told his young family about the house. Together they returned to the spot, but there was no house to be seen. Shortly after hearing this tale, Cobbold himself saw the house in one of the most dramatic sightings that we know about. George Waylett, the local pork butcher, was born in nearby Hessett in 1851. He reared pigs, and as Phil Sage informed me, his mother used to hold the unfortunate animals while he cut their throats. Then he would bring the carcasses over to his shop in Rougham. Cobbold would accompany him on his Saturday rounds, making deliveries with his pony and trap. On another warm June day, Cobbold and Waylett were heading south down Kingshall Street when the house suddenly materialised with a loud swooshing noise.

The pony uttered a kind of scream of terror and reared up, the butcher being thrown out of the back of the trap. Then it bolted, and eventually young Cobbold was able to bring it under control.

In those seconds he had had a clear view of a double fronted red brick house, three storied, of Georgian appearance, and a garden comprising a large oblong flower bed flanked with two circular beds, and three smaller oblong beds in front, with pansies and geraniums all in bloom, all edged with red bricks placed slantwise, also rose trees. Then a mist enveloped the house and it faded away. Waylett scrambled to his feet and exclaimed, "That ******** house! That's about the third time I've seen that happen!"

Despite Waylett's warnings, the young lad could not resist entering the field and looking in vain for traces left by the mystery building.

The Cobbold sighting was given special attention by Andrew Mackenzie in his excellent book about time slips, Adventures in Time [7]..

Basing his analysis upon research by the Bradfield St. George historian, Leonard Aves (now deceased) and a private researcher, Capt. Armstrong (RN), Mackenzie stated that he estimated that the sighting took place in 1908, four years earlier than Cobbold's own estimate. Moreover, he said that Cobbold himself estimated the episode to last between eight and ten minutes. Both of these data clearly contradict the content of Cobbold's article. Are we to accept that Cobbold did not know his age or the date of his sighting at the time he wrote the article? It seems unlikely. In addition, anybody reading that article with an open mind would clearly have concluded that the house would have been in view for no more than a minute or so.

THE BENTLEY-DAVIES CASE

In the 1940s, Edward Bentley was working for the Bury St Edmunds men's outfitter

Aubyn Davies, whose shop is still doing business today in St. John's Street. Bentley, aged about 20, used to go out with his manager in the late summer, distributing catalogues in the surrounding area. After harvest time, the farm workers had their bonuses and could afford new outfits. Davies was driving, and Bentley and another member of staff were delivering the catalogues. It was a warm, sunny day. They were heading south down Kingshall Street, when Bentley suddenly spotted a house off to the right, and quickly told Mr. Davies that they had missed one. Davies glanced back and reversed the car, but there was now no house to be seen. Bentley put the affair down to a mental aberration, but years later, when discussing the incident with his nephew, Chris Jensen Romer, he realised that he must have seen the ghost house. He pointed out to Chris and his team the exact location of the house near to Colville's Grove [4].

THE JEAN BATRAM CASE

On a cool but sunny Sunday afternoon in February 2007, Jean Batram and her husband Sydney (better known as "Johnnie"), a retired couple living in Great Barton, decided to go for a drive around some of the picturesque local villages. They headed south-east towards Rougham,

which Jean had never visited before and drove south down Kingshall Street. They had just passed the two bungalows opposite Colville's Grove when Jean spotted, on her left side, a large Georgian house. It lay across a newly harrowed field, in front of some woods. She pointed it out to Johnnie, who glanced over briefly, and said that as it was such a lovely house she would take a closer look at it on the way back.

After a pleasant drive, they returned along the same route.

However, there was no house to be seen. Jean was puzzled and asked Johnnie if he was certain they had come out on the same road. Of course, he was certain. It is the only road running south from Rougham.

Jean became increasingly worried over the coming weeks. She felt that they should report the incident to someone, but Johnnie disagreed vehemently. He declared that he had no wish to be subjected to ridicule, and would deny that he had seen the house himself. For eight months, Jean agonised over the matter.

Then, during a phone call to a friend of hers, Katarzyna Powell, she admitted that she had seen something very strange and didn't know what to do. To her surprise, Katarzyna replied, "Oh, you haven't seen the ghost house, have you?" Jean had had no idea that others had also witnessed the same phenomenon. Katarzyna went on to say that her daughter's boyfriend had also seen it, while out driving his van. Much against her husband's wishes, Jean then reported her story to the East Anglian Daily Times and it was subsequently published. [12] When Phil Sage contacted her, she agreed to an interview. Phil told me that he was impressed by her account, but that Johnnie had been openly sneering at her throughout the meeting and completely refused to back her up. (Johnnie died in 2012).

THE ROUGHAM MYSTERY

THE JEAN BATRAM CASE

The real problem was that while most other witnesses had seen a house on the west side of Kingshall Street, she had seen hers on the east side. Peter and Mary Cornish, are a valuable source of inside information about the local community, and outlined that there was a general disagreement amongst the Rougham community about which side the house appeared on, suggesting, perhaps, that other sightings on the east side had taken place but remained unreported. Jean and one of her sons were accompanied by Carl Grove to Rougham and she pointed out the place where she had seen the building. She was certain that it was a fairly large Georgian style house, and that it was standing somewhat to the right of Gypsy Lane, a narrow track that runs from Kingshall Street immediately south of the second bungalow. As Phil sage outlined to Carl, Gypsy Lane is the Greenway, a path originally employed by monks to transport wood to the Abbey at Bury St Edmunds. The Lane is an area subject to unusual events: ghostly figures, strange lighting phenomena, and other interesting occurrences. The photo shows the location, displaying the "X" drawn by Jean to mark the exact position of the house.

The author Carl Grove has been interested in the Rougham phenomena for several years and being that his wife was originally from Rougham had two similar experiences herself. On one occasion, while travelling in to work on a scooter, she saw men pushing a broken-down car a short distance ahead of her. They briefly went out of sight around a slight turn and when she reached it seconds later, there was no sign of men or car. Later she had another experience in the same place, this time involving an elderly lady cyclist. © Carl Grove, May, 2015 Bury St Edmunds, Suffolk, UK.

TIME-HOPPING: THE AMAZING STORY OF KEN WEBSTER

I recall a TV documentary about this case when Ken Webster, Nicola Baguely and Debbie Oakes returned home to find that their BBC microprocessor was switched on and some unseen force activated the green pulsating cursor. I wanted to include this as part of interdimensional aspect as this is a unique case of the interaction of technology and astral entity this also predates the use of EVP devices. [JPH]

Mr Marc Buck, a retired policeman and current ITC researcher in England, sent me a copy of his countryman Ken Webster's The Vertical Plane, which is out of print since the 1980s and very hard to get here in the States. So, thanks to Mark Buck, I finally got a chance to read Ken's landmark book this week and to write up a synopsis with a few of my own observations. Others have explored Webster's work in much greater depth... case in point

a forum that really digs into the subject (you can find 30-pages-and-counting of thoughtful dialog there), and a blog dedicated to "time slips" that discounts Webster's experiences as a hoax, and an insightful book review. My article below doesn't dig too deeply into Ken Webster's experiences (which I'm confident are valid interactions across time and dimensions), but I share a few thoughts that seem important to me. As with most of my writing, I just try to figure things out and put them in perspective.

Ken Webster's story: starts in late autumn 1984, in his cottage in the village of Dodleston, sitting on the border between England and Wales 30 miles south of Liverpool. Ken and his friends Debbie (Oakes) and Peter (Trinder) start experiencing strange goings-on in the cottage. First, there are footprints on the wall and writing on the floor, as though a dyslexic ghost gets things mixed up.

Then different kitchen items keep getting stacked up into tower formations. In the coming months the phenomena evolve into dozens of computer texts in Olde English from someone identifying himself as Lukas Wainman, who says he's currently living in the same cottage in "Dudleston," in the 1500s, late into the reign of King Henry VIII (1491-1547) who's currently married to his last wife, Queen Catherine Parr.

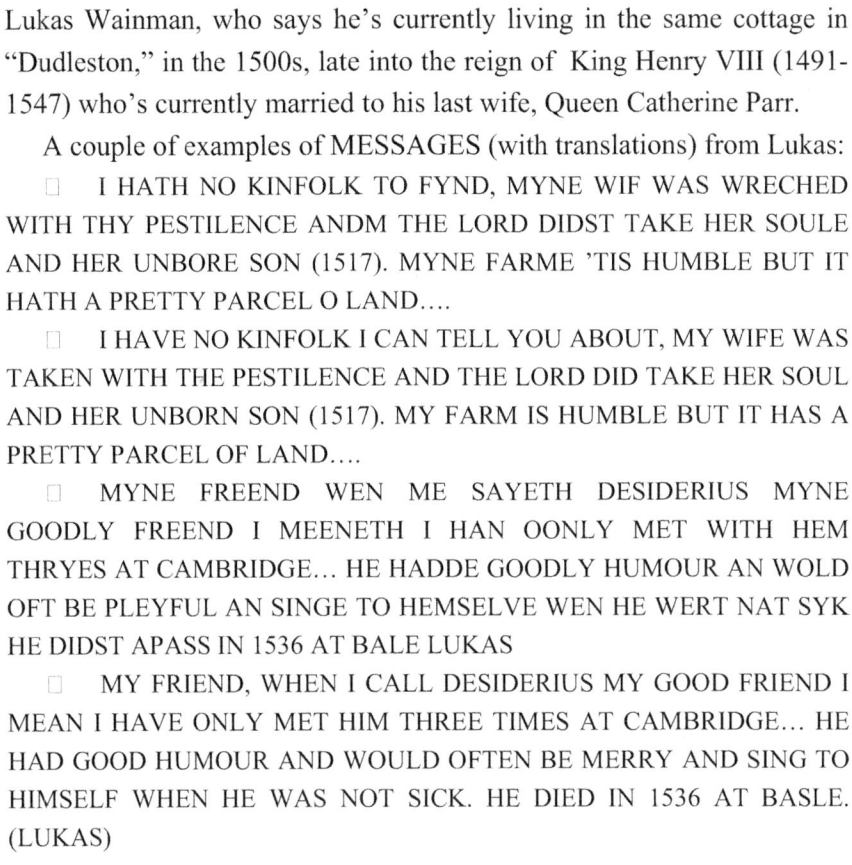

A couple of examples of MESSAGES (with translations) from Lukas:

☐ I HATH NO KINFOLK TO FYND, MYNE WIF WAS WRECHED WITH THY PESTILENCE ANDM THE LORD DIDST TAKE HER SOULE AND HER UNBORE SON (1517). MYNE FARME 'TIS HUMBLE BUT IT HATH A PRETTY PARCEL O LAND....

☐ I HAVE NO KINFOLK I CAN TELL YOU ABOUT, MY WIFE WAS TAKEN WITH THE PESTILENCE AND THE LORD DID TAKE HER SOUL AND HER UNBORN SON (1517). MY FARM IS HUMBLE BUT IT HAS A PRETTY PARCEL OF LAND....

☐ MYNE FREEND WEN ME SAYETH DESIDERIUS MYNE GOODLY FREEND I MEENETH I HAN OONLY MET WITH HEM THRYES AT CAMBRIDGE... HE HADDE GOODLY HUMOUR AN WOLD OFT BE PLEYFUL AN SINGE TO HEMSELVE WEN HE WERT NAT SYK HE DIDST APASS IN 1536 AT BALE LUKAS

☐ MY FRIEND, WHEN I CALL DESIDERIUS MY GOOD FRIEND I MEAN I HAVE ONLY MET HIM THREE TIMES AT CAMBRIDGE... HE HAD GOOD HUMOUR AND WOULD OFTEN BE MERRY AND SING TO HIMSELF WHEN HE WAS NOT SICK. HE DIED IN 1536 AT BASLE. (LUKAS)

What seems to be happening is this: Ken is a teacher who has access to a computer from the Maths and Computer Department at school, which he sets up in his home. A copy or spiritual template of that computer, or some other spirit-world communication device, somehow materializes in the 1500s home of Lukas, who sees it as a sort of mystical device with strange lights through which he can communicate with other-worldly beings (Ken and his friends from the 20th Century). Both computers (and devices) are in the same physical location, but four centuries apart.

That's what seems to be happening, but what's really happening, I believe, is something else. Maybe something simpler or maybe more complicated. I explain my theory at the end of the article, and you can decide.

Anyway, I think what Ken Webster had was an ITC bridge, similar to the ITC bridge of INIT… and I've come to believe lately that there are several key ingredients that make an ITC bridge possible. One is an "ITC disposition." I suspect Debbie Oakes and/or Ken Webster had an ITC disposition needed for the Dodleston bridge, the way that Maggy and Jules Harsch-Fischbach had an ITC disposition that fuelled our INIT bridge. Yang Fudse, a Chinese healer from the 3rd Century AD, told our INIT group:

In specially suited experimenters (to whom you wrongly refer as "successful") there develops a sort of "emotional lance" in the centre of their emotional consciousness, which "materializes" inaudible and invisible tones, signs, and pictures in your realm. People are usually born with this particular polarization of consciousness. Others may try as hard as they can, they will not get these results.

To this day, I have only a vague sense of what that actually means, but it's probably the best available definition of what I would call "an ITC disposition." So an ITC disposition is one prerequisite for an ITC bridge. A second prerequisite for an ITC bridge is a competent spirit team.

For our INIT group it was Timestream Spirit Group; for Ken and Debbie it's Group 2109, whom we'll talk about in a moment. That competent spirit group also has to include finer beings, or ethereal beings, who have the power and will to sustain and protect an ITC bridge.

Meanwhile, 20th Century Ken and 16th Century Lukas spend much of 1985 getting to know each other's worlds, lives, and personalities. Debbie starts having frequent encounters with Lukas in her dreams, and Lukas develops a crush on Debbie.

While Debbie is a charming, sensible, down-to-earth young woman here on Earth, she sometimes finds herself feeling like a flustered schoolgirl during her dream encounters with Lukas, who by modern standards would be considered a rather chauvinistic and domineering, sometimes bullying fellow... but with a kind heart. As a warm friendship develops across time, however, disruptive, contentious, or troublesome forces begin to enter the picture... forces on both ends of the bridge.

Troublesome Forces at the Other End of the Bridge

On Lukas's end of the bridge its "Group 2109," who seem to be coordinating the bridge or "the leems" as they call it. The 2109 group seem to be researchers from our future who are experimenting with time manipulation between 20th Century Earth and 16th Century Earth. (But who they really are, again, I try to explain at the end of this article.) Ken soon starts to get texts from "2109" as well from "Lukas." The 2109 texts are in a more modern or maybe even futuristic form of English... and the messages are not particularly friendly and heartfelt like the texts from Lukas.

This is one example of a text from 2109 group, who inform Ken and his friends that the project is being managed by higher forces, whom I suspect are finer spiritual beings who are closely monitoring, regulating, and protecting the bridge (the way that The Seven monitored, regulated, and protected the INIT bridge with Timestream spirit group). The 2109 group also inform Ken that "Lukas" is not the fellow's true identity. Ken soon starts to get texts from "2109" as well as from "Lukas."

Troublesome Forces at the Other End of the Bridge

This is one example of a text from 2109 group, who inform Ken and his friends that the project is being managed by higher forces, whom I suspect are finer spiritual beings who are closely monitoring, regulating, and protecting the bridge (the way that The Seven monitored, regulated, and protected the INIT bridge with Timestream spirit group). The 2109 group also inform Ken that "Lukas" is not the fellow's true identity.

This is one example of a text from 2109 group, who inform Ken and his friends that the project is being managed by higher forces, whom I suspect are finer spiritual beings who are closely monitoring, regulating, and protecting the bridge (the way that The Seven monitored, regulated, and protected the INIT bridge with Timestream spirit group). The 2109 group also inform Ken that "Lukas" is not the fellow's true identity.

His real name is Thomas, or Tomas. (Verbatim) WE ARE ALL CAPERBLE OF MAKING MISTAKES, ARN'T WE. YES, TELEPHONES … THE THINGS THAT YOU MAY CONSIDER ADVANCED COMMUNICATION – IF ONLY YOU COULD SEE WHAT IS TO COME!.WE, IN YOUR BETTER INTRESTS MADE SLIGHT 'ADJUSTMENT' TO YOUR CONVERSATIONS (– BUT PLEASE LET US CALL HIM BY HIS TRUE NAME)WITH THOMAS. WE ARE NOT ENTIRELY IN COMMAND OF THIS EXPERIMENT, SO WE CAN ONLY SAY THAT COMUNICATIONS WILL CEASE NO EARLYER THAN NOVEMBER (NOT NESSESERALY WITH THOMAS),AH, WE SEE, YOU WANT SOME PROOF FOR YOUR LITTLE COMIC!,WELL WE THINK YOU SHOULD FIRST TRY TO REVISE ON WHAT HAS ALREADY BEEN SAID. IF YOU TELL, US WHO IS 'ONE' THEN WE SHALL GIVE YOU 100% EVIDENCE FOR THE PEOPLE DIRECTLY INVESTIGATING YOUR PHENOMENA. 2109. This is typical of many messages from Group 2109, which are often cryptic and condescending… a fact that stirs up growing frustrations and suspicions among Ken and his friends. Such emotional bristling does not lend itself to a healthy, stable ITC bridge.

According to the information our INIT group was receiving from our own spirit group, Timestream, around the same time (maybe a few years later), who usually addressed us with respect and friendship and told us on one occasion, "It can only work when the vibrations of those present are in complete harmony, and when their aims and intentions are pure." Group 2109 did not seem to foster that kind of harmony and purity of aims and intentions.

Troublesome Forces on This End of the Bridge

Enter investigators from the Society for Psychical Research (SPR). Typical of many SPR investigators, John Bucknall and Dave Welch are a skeptical team. They suspect from that onset that Ken's claims and experiences are probably (or at least very possibly) a hoax Lukas senses troubles right away:

☐ "Aren't they scholars from our beloved Oxford? Why do they come to see my 'leems'? What cause do these men serve by doing so?" (Chapter 25)

Ken Webster had early hopes about the SPR investigators:

"14 May (1985). Mr John Bucknall rang.

He was, he said, the SPR field officer, which John Stiles had promised. I took to him instinctively, he sounded young, intelligent and precise.   I felt relieved in the way that a patient often finds relief in simply knowing that the doctor will call.

John Bucknall, so I conjectured, with a few questions and a couple of evenings sitting quietly with Debbie in a sealed house, would proclaim us all extremely sane. He might even write a report for the Society describing just how valuable the case was." (Chapter 17)

That optimism soon changed. Ken wrote: "Dave Welch huffed and puffed his way to and fro with a reel-to-reel tape recorder, bags of wires, rolls of sticky tape and other assorted items.

John Bucknall detailed the plan for the evening. In the studio, they would set up a 'listening post' with a microphone run out of the window across the kitchen roof and through a slightly open skylight into the kitchen itself.

John Bucknall detailed the plan for the evening. In the studio, they would set up a 'listening post' with a microphone run out of the window across the kitchen roof and through a slightly open skylight into the kitchen itself. They would set it running and wait in the living room.... John Bucknall was trying not to chain-smoke. He emphasized that many of these sorts of phenomena are entirely fraudulent or are massive elaborations upon some quite explainable occurrence. Was he here to investigate or to name the guilty persons?" (Chapter 17) My take? ITC is a difficult process here on Earth. A stable bridge requires trust, honesty, friendship, and love, but humans by nature aren't always trusting, honest, friendly, and loving.

Troublesome Forces on This End of the Bridge

When suspicious, fearful, people get involved with an ITC bridge, the bridge destabilizes and disappears. Kind of a "Catch-22" scenario. That was probably the case with Ken Webster's ITC bridge, which seemed to work best when the SPR investigators weren't around.

In other cases, ITC bridges will invariably falter when researchers are dishonest, insincere, self-seeking, or malicious. That wasn't the case with Ken Webster and the Dodleston bridge, but it seems to be a kind of rule-of-thumb for ITC research everywhere.

There must be trust, honesty, friendship, and love... the kinds of things you'd probably find prominently in the hearts and psyches of people like Debbie Oakes and Maggy Fischbach.

Two Unanswered Questions and Best Guesses

First, was there an actual, physical communication device in Lukas's cottage 4 centuries ago on physical Earth, or did all of that happen in an astral template of the Earth? I suspect the latter. I have come to believe that every material thing in our material universe, whether a molecule or a rock or a tree or a person or a planet... everything has a spiritual template. Moreover, that template exists while the physical thing exists, and it continues to exist after the physical thing dies or is destroyed.

So the ITC bridge between Ken and Lukas wasn't built between two physical locations on physical Earth at different times, but between Ken's physical location and the astral (spiritual) location where Lukas, Thomas, Group 2109, and other personalities are still living since the death of their carnal bodies.

From our perspective of three-dimensional living, we could say that Ken's physical location and Lukas's spiritual location are superimposed over each other... just as physical Earth and Earth's spiritual templates are superimposed over each other. At one point in the book, Lukas is taken away to prison. Ken and Debbie are alarmed and worried that Lukas has died in prison. I suspect the truth is that Lukas can't die, because he's not a carnal human living a carnal drama; he is an astral spirit who's reliving patterns of earthly dramas that keep spinning in the astral world or spiritual template in which he's now living. Here's a MESSAGE (and translation) from a fellow named "John" that arrived while Lukas was in prison:

THE SHERYFF DOES ASKE THAT THOU SPEKE TO HYM WYTH THY SELVEN SHEWN TO HYS EYE FOR THY PURPOSE RATHER THROUGH THE COMUTER WHICHE HE HATH NO SIGHT FOR ELLES THE COMUTER MUSTE BEE TAKEN TO LUCAS IN BOWGHTONE PRYSUN OR NANTWHICHE IF HE BEE THYR NOWE TO SHEW HE SPAKE TROUTHS BUTT TIS NOT ETHE TO MOOV THY DEVICE FOR YT SEEMS TO MISAPERE WHEN ENY HAVE TRYD ONLIE WHEN LUCAS BEE HERE DOES YT SHYNE AS SOLYD I CRY THY TELLYNGS TO POST JOHN..

Two Unanswered Questions and Best Guesses

The sheriff does ask that you speak to him in person rather than through the computer, which he can't see. Otherwise, the computer must be taken to Lukas in Boughton prison or Nantwich, if he is there now, to show that he spoke the truth. But it is not easy to move the device as it seems to disappear when any have tried. Only when Lukas is here does it appear solid. I beg a quick reply so I may go to him, John. This message sounds rather insane in this carnal world Earth that we inhabit. But in an astral world, or a spiritual template of Earth, it makes more sense. Lukas might have been inconveniently carted off to prison for a while in one of those astral dramas that keep spinning around in that shadow world. But the computer-template-device (leems) that's been materialized by Group 2109 and their supervising team in Lukas's astral cottage has to stay in the cottage... and since the device is synchronized to or customized for Lukas, it becomes less solid and less operable when Lukas isn't present. So... Lukas is shortly released from prison and brought home so he can continue his ITC work until the bridge is scheduled (by the finer spiritual supervisors, whoever they are) to close down sometime around November earth time.

This kind of scenario is certainly not easy to follow

and grasp with our carnal minds, but I think it starts to make more sense as we begin to understand our spiritual nature… which has always been wrapped up in mystery for us noble-savage humans who spend our lives running around and bumping into each other on planet Earth. There's a bigger, multidimensional picture that ITC researchers are starting to get a better glimpse of. Hopefully humanity will be patient with us as, together, we try to figure it all out.

Second, how were all of those messages entered into the computer-template-device in Lukas's 16th Century cottage? Did Lukas and the others have to sit in front of a keyboard and hunt-and-peck the messages painstakingly with their fingers… the way that we carnal humans have to do

in this dense world?… or is there some means of converting their thoughts into words? Again, I suspect the latter.

While Ken Webster's Dodleston bridge and INIT's Timestream bridge were operating late last century, an even more famous bridge was underway at Scole, England. The Scole group asked their spirit friends on one occasion how they were able to speak with such loud, clear voices that filled the room where the researchers sat in a circle. One spirit replied:

"We don't actually speak. We think our message, and there are others here who, by some miracle, are able to convert our thoughts into the words you hear in your world."

The same was probably true for Ken Webster and for our INIT group. When our spirit friends spoke to us through phones or radios, or when they sent text messages through our computers, they didn't speak or type the way we do here on Earth.

They simply had to think their messages, and there were teams of experts around them in the spirit world who had the knowledge, ability, and will to convert those thoughts into sounds, text, and images that would be meaningful to us dense, carnal humans on this dense, carnal Earth.

That's the gist of ITC communications at the present time of human evolution. It's still a little dense, but we're all doing the best we can. As we humans become more astute or multidimensional or more acclimated to our dealings with the invisible worlds around us, ITC will become a more fluid process. Of that, I have no doubt.

Further Information: *Macy Afterlife The Beacon..https://macyafterlife.com*

THREADS OF TIME

THE RENDLESHAM FOREST INCIDENT

Considered as being one of the most recognised UFO cases in the UK, also been labelled as "Britain's Roswell." The Rendlesham case has gained extensive exposure on numerous TV documentaries and print media coverage. I would identify the incident as a time travel case as the entities that made contact via a telepathic coded message to Sgt Jim Penniston may have been time travellers from the distant future or a parallel dimension. The event took place close to the U.S Airforce base RAF Woodbridge, Suffolk, England; this is a brief overview of the event. Moreover, prior to the Rendlesham case, other anomalous sightings have been documented within the proximity of RAF Woodbridge and RAF Bentwaters. These accounts of earlier sightings are listed on tracymonger.wordpress.com, which contain examples of anomaly related incidents around East Anglia, which also include unidentified aerial phenomena cases dating from 1956 at Lakenheath-Bentwaters, also two in the Woodbridge area on the 9th June 1961 then later in October 1965. RAF Bentwaters was very close to RAF Woodbridge, both sites were classed as a single base facility. Woodbridge was selected by the Royal Air Force in 1943, described as being 'nearly fog-free and having no obstructions for miles', however more than a few thousand trees had to be cleared from Rendlesham Forest to construct the airfield.

During WW2, the base was used for receiving distressed aircraft returning from raids over Germany.

With the onset of the Cold War, the Ministry of Defence made RAF Woodbridge available to the USAF in early 1952. The Rendlesham UFO sighting was reported on 26 December 1980, around 03:00 a.m. . . .[Colonel Halt recorded the incident in his memo for the Ministry of Defence report as taking place on the 27 December]. Airman First Class John Burroughs originally saw the lights hovering above the location known as the East Gate which leads off into Rendlesham Forest.

He immediately alerted his supervisor Staff Sergeant Bud Steffens, considering a possible downed aircraft of unknown origin, Steffens called for assistance. They were later joined by Sgt Jim Pennsiton and Airman First Class Edward Cabansag; he briefed Penniston and Cabansag taking into account that it may have been an aircraft that crash-landed.

The Encounter

Later, Sgt Penniston, Ed Cabansag, and John Burroughs drove towards the potential crash site, but had to access the target location by foot. As the men got closer, they saw a strange glowing object, metallic in appearance, with coloured lights. In addition, within close range of the object the radio equipment began to malfunction. Cabansag was asked to relay messages to the control centre; at this point, the radio communications to the CSC – [Central Security Control,] began to disintegrate. In the report, the team later described how the air was full of static electricity, along with an unusual tingling feeling on hair, skin and clothing. In addition, the perception that time had been distorted, everything was slowing down, and the whole area was enclosed in total silence. As Sgt Penniston moved closer towards the beam of light, he discovered that the source came from a dark triangular shaped object. Being a trained observer, he could identify all types of Eastern Bloc and NATO military aircraft. However at this point he was unable to determine the origin of this type of craft. Then the object began to transmit a sequence of lights, which flashed recurrently on either side. Sgt Penniston described the whole structure as looking metallic, then added, 'there was a red light which flashed intermittently, no landing gear, no exhaust, and no windows'.

'There was a sequence of hieroglyphics and cryptic patterns located at the base section.' [*50]. Immediately, Sgt Penniston took out his notebook and made a brief sketch of the craft, estimating the dimension to be about 2 meters high and about 3 meters in width. The series of patterns beneath the craft were, 5 to 6ins [152.4mm] high. The markings consisted of a triangle and other unidentifiable geometric shapes

The surface section containing the markings, equalled to course grade sandpaper in comparison to the ceramic type qualities found on the upper sections. Suddenly, Sgt Penniston was engulfed by intense light. 'At this point I thought I was going to explode or disintegrate', he took the defensive position by lying on the ground and taking cover. Moments later, he looked up watching the object hovering above the treetops. Then within a few seconds, it disappeared. The following day, while in his room, Sgt Penniston was inundated with flashbacks, which included images of what he described as a stream of 0's and 1's. On reflection, he accredited this as some form of telepathic communication. Evidently, by description, the 0's and 1's would have been binary code. Some scientists believe that binary code is a universal system of contacting extra-terrestrial life. Back in 1974 an experiment known as the Arecibo Message, was compiled in binary. The content included components on the human race and basic references to life on earth. The message was compiled by Frank Drake and Carl Sagan, and later broadcasted in the direction of the M-13 star cluster, relaying a single time frame transmission from the Arecibo radio telescope in Puerto Rico at a frequency of 2,380 MHz.

Moreover, Ronald Mallet, Professor Emeritus of Physics at the University of Connecticut said. 'If ever you wanted to send a message through time, you could do it by using binary code'. Prof Mallet highlighted this concept when researching the properties of subatomic particles and neutrons.

He found that the arrangement on some elements would point up while others point down. The positional values of the subatomic particles, if encoded, represent negative or positive states.

Perhaps if modified; these values may be translated into some aspect of binary code. Convinced that these messages were linked to the night of the incident, Sgt Penniston wrote down the sequence of code as it came through.

On completion, the transcription was sixteen pages long. Binary code was not common knowledge back in 1980, unless you were a computer scientist or computer operator, or perhaps some schools in the late 1970s, may have covered brief elements of computer studies that included the conversion of decimal numbers to binary. One of the supplementary questions would have been at the time, what is binary code used for? Binary code is part of the text form used for computer processor instructions. Using the two-symbol system of 0 and 1 the binary code assigns a pattern of binary digits (bits) to each character, instruction, etc. For example, a binary string of eight bits can represent any of 256 possible values and can therefore represent a variety of different items, which eventually is converted into code and text [*51]. These 0s and 1s did not bear any significance or translatable value to him so he filed the book away. However, 30 years later while meeting researchers from a TV production company, as both Jim Penniston and the TV crew paused to establish time and dates from the notebook.

THREADS OF TIME

While skimming through the pages, one of the production crew noticed the sequence of zero's and one's, and was excited by the additional element of content and offered to pass the details on for an expert to decipher the codes. Jim highlighted in his previous book *'Encounter in Rendlesham Forest: published in April 2014'* Stated that he shared a small part of the codes with only a few trusted individuals.

Taken from pages 1 to 16 EXPLORATION of Humanity 666 8100 52.0942532N 13.131269W (Hy Brasil) CONTINUOUS FOR PLANETARY ADVAN??? (transmission fragmented) FOURTH COORDINATE CONTINUED UQS CbPR BEFORE 16.763177N 89.117768W (Cazaccl, Belize) 34.800272N 111.943567W (Sedona, Arizona) 29.977836N 31.13:649E (Great Pyramid in Giza, Egypt) 14.701505S 75.167043W (Nazca Lns in Peru) 36.256845N 117.100632E (Tal Shan Dii, «,in) 37.1101 95N 25.3722A1F'. (Potara at Temple of Apollo in Naxos, Greece) EYES OF YOUR EYES ORIGIN 52.O942532IJ LL131269W (EyBras:l)

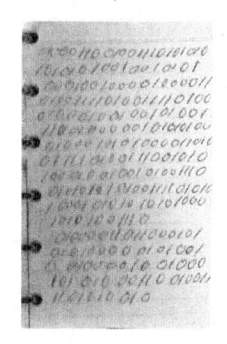

ORIGIN YEAR 8100 The breakdown of the message: Time is the fourth coordinate of (x,y,z,t) "Origin 52.0942532N 13.131269W" "Origin Year 8100" The key element of the message could be "Origin Year 8100" which initiated the idea, that the occupants who transmitted the codes were in fact time travellers from the year 81000.

The other coordinates listed include 16.763177N 89.117768W (Cazaccl, Belize or Caracol an ancient Mayan site)................ 34.800272N 111.943567W (Sedona, Arizona, part of the Sinagua culture, cliff settlements containing petroglyphs) 29.977836N 31.13:649E (Great Pyramid in Giza, Egypt) 14.701505S 75.167043W (Nazca Lns in Peru) 36.256845N 117.100632E (Tal Shan Dii, «, in) these coordinates relate to ancient sites and known portals across the world.

According to the interpretation, *Eyes for your Eyes* could be the designation of the mission for the 6000-year-old interdimensional travellers- "to see for themselves" their parallel dimension of 1980. Curiously enough, the coordinates listed also indicate locations of ancient sites and known portals across the world. I have discovered while examining Ordnance Survey maps around the east of England. There are two prehistoric earthworks or tumuli within a radius of Rendlesham forest.

These are, Shottisham Monument Complex: 3km SW of Rendlesham Forest, and a tumulus near Upper Hollesey Common 2.6 km SW from Rendlesham forest. Researchers, who study perspectives on the prehistoric mind, and culture, have suggested that ancient people were more tuned into their environment or in general terms had a sixth sense and felt that specific places had a certain presence or 'power'. Moreover, alternative archaeologists and dowsers, speculate the possible existence of portals to other dimensions, which might be located, even on minor ancient sites. For example, the Rollright stones located on the Oxfordshire/Warwickshire border in England, researchers found that the stones generate minor traces of beta and gamma radiation. Moreover, other similar sites may emit a magnetic force, as for example the Dragon Project, initiated by Paul Devereux in 1977-87 the main objective was to detect and quantify earth energies. One of the main aspects of the investigation was to detect forms of magnetism, ionizing radiation, and ultrasound within Prehistoric sites. Don Robins, a consultant on the project with a background in chemistry stated that stone circles are able to emit varied types of radiation at varied levels. Another researcher on the project used an ultrasound detector and found high levels of ultrasound emitting from the Rollright stone just before dawn on a foggy day. Perhaps, certain parts of Rendlesham forest may have concealed points that transmit natural frequencies.

On the decoded message included the coordinates: 52.0942532N 13.131269W that indicated a locality called Hy Brasil, situated 200 miles off the west coast of Ireland. In contrasted versions of the etymology of the name includes, Hy Brussel but in Irish tradition it is thought to come from the Gaelic Uí Breasail (meaning "descendants (i.e., clan) of Breasal"), one of the ancient clans of north-eastern Ireland. cf. Old Irish: Í: island; bres: beauty, worth, great, mighty."[*52]

Hy Brasil: Described as the Celtic Atlantis, this mythical island has been pursued for centuries by explorers. Some have documented that an island, which suddenly appears out of the sea, shrouded in mist then fades away as soon if anyone manages to get within reach.

Hy Brasil has been charted since 1325 A.D; *Derivative work: AFBorchert (talk) 1572_Europa_Ortelius.jpg: Ortelius, Public domain, via Wikimedia Commons*

Rudimentary illustrations show an enclosure of rocks. The earliest available detailed chart dates to the 1600s that indicate a small green land mass in the middle of the sea. Some researchers claim that Hy Brasil exists, but in possible or "mirror dimension." To add further, the island could be an inversion of our existing dimension, which may have entities that co-exist in this realm.

On analysis, most of the UFO accounts around the west coast of Ireland have reports from witnesses describing triangular shaped flying objects. The dates of the reports originate from varied time frames. However, it appears to be a coincidence, being that Hy Brasil is located directly to the west of Ireland; could the sightings of triangular craft hold a connection to the Rendlesham incident? In the early hours of the 29th December 1980, deputy base commander, Lieutenant Colonel Charles Halt, visited the site along with a team of servicemen. They took radiation readings of the triangular imprints in the soil and the surrounding area using an AN/PDR-27, a standard U.S. military radiation survey meter. On conclusion, MOD staff assessed Halt's official report, stating that the radiation readings are "significantly higher than the average background readings.

THE WOOLPIT CASE, SUFFOLK, ENGLAND

The Woolpit Case appears to be an incident that relates to interdimensional travel. There are no other updates, since the documented recording, which originated in the 12th century. Due the source of the original story which later developed into a mesh of interpretations.

So far, no other contemporary investigation is ongoing, as most scholars have collated or attempted to decipher the original accounts as to examine other possible explanations.

The Encounter:
One day at harvest time, according to William of Newburgh during the reign of King Stephen (r. 1135–1154)

[1] The villagers of Woolpit discovered two children, a brother and sister, beside one of the wolf pits [A wolf pit was a deep pit into which carrion was thrown to attract wolves, and then covered over with branches] that gave the village its name. [4][b] Their skin was green, they spoke an unknown language, and their clothing was unfamiliar. Recorded by Ralph of Coggeshall (1207–1218) who was the sixth abbot of Coggeshall Abbey, summarises that the children were taken to the home of Richard de Calne. Ralph and William agree that the pair refused all food for several days even though they were tormented by great hunger. Not until they came across some raw broad beans, which they consumed eagerly. The children gradually adapted to normal food and in time lost their green colour. [1] The boy, who appeared to be the younger of the two, became sickly and died shortly after he and his sister were baptised. The girl adjusted to her new life, but she was considered to be "rather loose and wanton in her conduct".[2] After she learned to speak English, the girl explained that she and her brother had come from Saint Martin's Land, a subterranean world inhabited by green people.

The girl described that she and her brother came from a land where the sun never shone and the light was like twilight. The children were unable to describe their arrival to Woolpit village.

The only recollection was they had been herding their father's cattle when they heard a loud noise (according to William, the bells of Bury St Edmunds [9]) and suddenly found themselves by the wolf pit where they were found. Ralph says that they had become lost when they followed the cattle into a cave and, after being guided by the sound of bells, eventually emerged into our land.[1]

According to Ralph, the girl was employed for many years as a servant of the local landowner Richard de Calne, and considered the girl to be "very wanton and impudent."

William of Newburgh documented that she eventually married a man from King's Lynn, located 40 miles (64 km) from Woolpit, where she was still living shortly before he wrote. Based on his research into Richard de Calne's family history, the astronomer and writer Duncan Lunan has concluded that the girl was given the name "Agnes" and that she married a royal official named Richard Barre.[10]

The only near-contemporary accounts are contained in William of Newburgh's Historia rerum Anglicarum. Ralph of Coggeshall's Chronicum Anglicanum also recorded the case between 1189 and 1220. Between then and their rediscovery in the mid-19th century, the green children seem to surface only in a passing mention in William Camden's Britannia in 1586 [1]. In Bishop Francis Godwin's fantastical The Man in the Moone that was written in the early 17th century mentions 'green children'[3] both of which William of Newburgh's account is cited, other than those sources, contemporary researchers view these as fictional folk tales or a distorted account of a historical event.

Along with stories of encounters with fairies, moreover, a contemporary enquiry could be 'were the green children of Woolpit extraterrestial entities?' Neither Ralph of Coggeshall nor William of Newburgh offer an explanation for the "strange and prodigious" event as William calls it. Some modern historians have the same reticence:

"I consider the process of worrying over the suggestive details of these wonderfully pointless miracles in an effort to find natural or psychological explanations of what 'really,'……

if anything, happened, to be useless to the study of William of Newburgh or, for that matter, of the Middle Ages", says Nancy Partner, author of a study of 12th-century historiography [11].

Nonetheless, such explanations continue to be sought and two approaches have dominated explanations of the mystery of the green children. The first is that the narrative descends from folklore, describing an imaginary encounter with the inhabitants of a "fairy Otherworld"[1].

In a few early[1] as well as modern readings, this other world is extraterrestrial, and the green children alien beings[10].

Additional Explanation:

The second is that it is a garbled account of a real event,[1] although it is impossible to be certain whether the story as recorded is an authentic report given by the children or an "adult invention"[12]. His study of accounts of children and servants fleeing from their masters led Charles Oman to conclude that "there is clearly some mystery behind it all [the story of the green children], some story of drugging and kidnapping". [13] Jeffrey Jerome Cohen offers a different kind of historical explanation, arguing that the story is an oblique account of the racial difference between the contemporary English and the indigenous Britons. [14].

Many Flemish immigrants arrived in eastern England during the 12th century, and they were persecuted after Henry II became king in 1154; a large number of them were killed near Bury St Edmunds in 1173 at the Battle of Fornham fought between Henry II and

Robert de Beaumont, 3rd Earl of Leicester. Paul Harris has suggested that the green children's Flemish parents perished during a period of civil strife and that the children may have come from the village of Fornham St Martin, slightly to the north of Bury St Edmunds, where a settlement of Flemish fullers existed at that time.

[1] Brian Haughton considers Harris's explanation to be plausible, and the one most widely accepted,[21] although not without doubt. As an example, he suggests it is unlikely that an educated local man like Richard de Calne would not have recognised the language spoken by the children as being Flemish [22]. To emphasise the fact if there were Flemish immigrants living within a close range of Woolpit village, there is no doubt even a few sentences in the Flemish language (described as a Belgian variant of Dutch) could have been recognised by Richard de Calne.

Regarding the extraterrestrial theory, Author Duncan Lunan suggested the children might have been transported by accident from a device called a "matter transmitter" that malfunctioned. Moreover, planet they were from may have been in constant twilight, and located on a peripheral location from its own sun , additionally the food sources on their planet were responsible for their green pallor.

Time Travel Aspect:

Part of the account is they came out of a cave, is one of many folklore accounts in a similar vein. For example Gerald of Wales (Archdeacon of Brecon 1146 – c. 1223) tells a similar story of a boy who, after escaping his master, "encountered two pigmies who led him through an underground passage into a beautiful land with fields and rivers, but not lit by the full light of the sun." [13] Another speculation that has been suggested, could the two children been time travellers?

It has the hallmarks of a timeslip, as they may have arrived from a future Earth probably five centuries in which even modern English would be incomprehensible to us let alone any one in 12th century England who were speaking Early Middle English, or could it be another verbal syntax from a parallel dimension? However, the story maybe genuine but exaggerated, most medieval chroniclers were mainly clerics and any tales that would be viewed as a 'miracle' and related accounts would be documented to emphasise the power of religious belief.

BIBLIOGRAPHY

BIBLIOGRAPHY

Brief Outline of Theories: Pages 4-7

[*1]Frien Betty (2017, October 25) Time Travel is a Possibility https://owlcation.com/stem/So-You-Want-To-Time-Travel

Kind permission from Betty Frein for the article, other links to articles can be found on https://hubpages.com/@annkf

[*2] Cartlidge, E. (2015, February 5). Photons simulate time travel in the lab. Retrieved from https://physicsworld.com/a/photons-simulate-time-travel-in-the-lab. partial reference

[*3] partially from Dickinson K (2019 June 10) Are scientists on the brink of discovering a mirror universe/https://bigthink.com/surprising-science/mirror-universe/ partial reference

[*4] . https://phys.org/news/2006-04-professor-human-century.html

Bold Street, Liverpool: Pages 8-12

[*5] Source: Liverpool Echo: Youth Slipped in 1967, Tom Slemen
https://www.liverpoolecho.co.uk/news/liverpool-news/tom-slemens-tales-liverpool-timeslips-3372751

The Brighton Vortex: Pages 13-15

[*6] https://www.theargus.co.uk/news/10414195.vortex-to-another-dimension-reported-in-brighton/

[*7] http://shop.hauntedcuriosities.com/Vortex-to-Secret-Masonic-Meetings-Discovered-0631307.htm

with kind permission from Deedee Doughty.

[*8] https://en.wikipedia.org/wiki/Pepper_Pot,_Brighton

Time slips relating to WW II

World War 2 Timeslip. London Underground: Pages 22-23
[*9, *10 *11] cited from : http://www.deathclicks.com/2010/11/time-slip-at-waterloo-station.html.

They experienced an air raid from the future: Pages 27-28
[*12] derived the original article by Cynthia McKanzie –:
http://www.messagetoeagle.com/three-fascinating-old-time-travel-cases-these-people-say-they-saw-the-future-past/

The Secret Garden: Leeds, West Yorkshire, UK : Pages 29-30
[*13] Intro and summary by JP Harris [*14] Ghost Reporter: The Files page 135. By Paul Gater, Anecdotes Publishing.

Telephone Call: Page 31
[*15]Tom Slemen : accessed, 14/05/2018, www.qsl.net/w5www/timeslips.html.
Tom Slemen 2001

Transmissions:
Short Wave Radio Incident: Pages 35-37
Article by Jerry Decker- www.keelynet.com

Sid Hurwich The Man Who Could Freeze Time: Pages 38-42
Source: www.messagetoeagle.com/mystery-of-sid-hurwich-and-his-time-altering-machine-that-could-freeze-time-Cynthia McKanzie – October 23, 2015 [*16]

Smith, Terence (4 July 1976). [*17]"Hostages Freed as Israelis Raid Uganda Airport; Commandos in 3 Planes Rescue 105-Casualties Unknown Israelis Raid Uganda Airport and Free Hijackers' Hostages". The New York Times. Retrieved 4 July 2009.

Bath Time Machine: Pages 43-48

Source: On The Edge, series No 15 Terry Le Riche Walters, 29.03.2010

www.dailymotion.com

Source On The Edge, series No18 Part1 Rev Lionel Fanthorpe, 10.08.2010

www.dailymotion.com

The Vatican Time Machine: Pages 49-53

The Vatican Time Machine:

[*18] Stuart Kirkpatrick on www.coolinterestingstuff.com

[*19] Eddie. "https://worldtruth.tv/wikileaks-cias-most-secret-weapon-is-time-machine-from-vatican/." worldtruth.tv.
https://worldtruth.tv/author/chloe1127/.

[*20]David E.H., Jones (1982), The Inventions of Daedalus: A Compendium of Plausible Schemes,

W.H. Freeman & Company, ISBN 0-7167-1412-[*21] [wikipedia.org/wiki/Archaeoacousticscite:note-28]

Dimensional Slips

Antarctic Case: Pages 54-56
Source:www.thelivingmoon.com/47brotherthebig/01archives/Time_P ravda.htm Olga Zharina 02, 2004.www.pravda.ru/ [*22]

Russian Time Travel Experiments: Pages 57-61
Cited from source
http://english.pravda.ru/science/19/94/379/12190_experiment.html.
Kind permission from Dmitry Sudakov.... www.pravda.ru [*23]

The Plane that Vanished: Page 62
The Epoch Times: Macisaac,Tara: Plane Said to Vanish, Reappear 10 Minutes Later: Time Slip? August 12, 2015 Updated: March 27, 2016 accessed

[*24].. 21/10/2017.Source: www.theepochtimes.com/plane-said-to-vanish-reappear-10-minutes-later-time-slip_1715532.html

Seville, Spain Interdimensional Slip : Pages 63-64
Seville, Spain: Interdimensional Slip
Scott ,Corrales INEXPLICATA-THE JOURNAL OF HISPANIC UFOLOGY : http://inexplicata.blogspot.com/2012/04/spain-possible-abduction-or.html29,04, 2012

Did Large Hadron Collider create time travel?
Machine shut down after plane vanishes' : Pages 67-69
Austin Jon https://www.express.co.uk/news/weird/696186/Did-Large-Hadron-Collider-create-TIME-TRAVEL-Machine-shut-down-after-plane-vanishespublished: 07:44, Wed, Aug 17, 2016

The Philadelphia experiment: Pages 70-77
Editor JPH [*25]
[*26]Crystal,Ellie
https://www.crystalinks.com/PhiladelphiaExperiment.html
Accessed, 20.04.2018.

Die Glocke; Hitler's Time Machine: Pages 78-84
[*27]Paraphrased source
http://www.crystalinks.com/nazibell.html 22.05.2018

The Iraq StarGate: Pages 85-88
[*28] Sanders, B. (2020, January 13). BERNIE SANDERS ON IRAQ. Retrieved from https://feelthebern.org/bernie-sanders-on-iraq/

[*29], D. (2020, January 13). Anglo-Iraqi War. Retrieved from http://dbpedia-live.openlinksw.com/resource/Iraq_1941

[*30] Michael Paul Johnson , . (2020, January 13). World English Bible, Retrieved from https://worldenglish.bible/

The Strange Case of Rudolph Fentz: Pages 89-91
[*31] Intro by J.P Harris and [*32] Berry, C. (2015, January 1). Rudolph Fentz legend 'Who is Rudolph Fentz. Retrieved from Online,
https://crberryauthor.com/2016/06/09/time-travel-in-times-square-the-strange-case-of-rudolph-fentz/

[*33]Christopher Berry's short story on the Rudolph Fentz legend 'Who is Rudolph Fentz? 'can be found on the following link: https://crberryauthor.wordpress.com/the-million-eyes-short-stories/

It was the first of the Million Eyes Short Stories to be published. You can also find 'Who is Rudolph Fentz? in the Scribble Magazine , Issue 68 (2015).

Portals

Timeslip into the Future Scholes, Kirklees, West Yorkshire, UK
Pages: 94-95-
Randles, Jenny Page 172-Supernatural Pennines, 2002 Robert Hale Publishing, London.]

Manchester Time Slip: 95-97
[*34] [Randles, Jenny Pages 102/103-Supernatural Pennines, 2002 Robert Hale Publishing, London.]

Loch Ness Timeslip: Pages 102-103
[*35]] C.R Berry, https://crberryauthor.wordpress.com/2015/04/02/the-truth-about-loch-ness-time-travel-and-the-taos-hum/
[*36] Alien Energy, Collins Andrew, Published by Eagle Wing Books
.[*37] Maurice Townsend 2006,
http://www.assap.ac.uk/newsite/htmlfiles/Geology.html

Are there any theories behind time slips and interdimensional travel?: Pages 104-115
[*38] Vaidman ,L - 2002 – Many-Worlds Interpretation of Quantum Mechanics (Stanford) [*39] Carl Sagan Ponders Time Travel". NOVA. PBS. December 10, 1999. Retrieved April 26, 2017. [*40] Frank Arntzenius; Tim Maudlin (December 23, 2009), "Time Travel and Modern Physics", Stanford Encyclopaedia of Philosophy [*41]

[*41] Mark Baard (September 5, 2005), Time Travelers Welcome at MIT, Wired, retrieved June 18, 2018 [*42] Franklin, Ben A. (March 11, 1982). "The night the planets were aligned with Baltimore lunacy". The New York Times. Archived from the original on 2008-12-06.[*43] [*44]"Welcome the People from the Future. March 9, 1982". Ad in Artforum p. 90.   [*45]. Ball, Philip - New pursuit of Schrödinger's cat – Prospect, retrieved 20 July 2014

[*46] Wikipedia https://en.wikipedia.org/wiki/Singlet_state

[*47] Kristine, Moore,. "Time Passing May Be An Illusion, According To The Block Universe Theory, As Past, Present, And Future Co-Exist". Online www.yahoo.com/news/time-passing-may-illusion-according-031343836.html 27 Sep. 2018.

[*48] Vortexes Online www.ranker.com/list/how-to-open-a-portal-to-another-dimension/jodi-smith

The Rougham Mystery : Pages 116-125

1. Moberly, C. A. E. & Jourdain, E. F. An Adventure, 1911 and many later editions. Although

most researchers refer to this as one case, there were actually three separate events, the first

involving both witnesses, and the second, a few months later, experienced by Miss Jourdain on her own. Then, in 1908, while taking photos, Miss Jourdain had a brief view of a gateway melting away. The authors also found similar stories from other witnesses, including a family which had lived near the gardens for two years. After moving away they returned for a visit and it became clear that they had never actually seen the contemporary Versailles during their residency.

2. Bennett, E. Apparitions and Haunted Houses, 1939. Recorded many hundreds of cases sent in to the BBC during the 1930s. Obviously it is a moot point whether time slips should be placed in the same category as ghost phenomena, though there is clearly an overlap.

3. For example, John Fairley and Simon Welfare in Arthur C. Clarke's Chronicles of the Strange and Mysterious, 1987, declare confidently that "the solution to this mystery may lie in Miss Wynne's original account... did her unfamiliarity with the local landscape cause her to make a mistake on her return visit... leading them to confuse one location with another?" (p. 115) 4. Chris quotes on his website http://jerome23.wordpress.com/tag/rougham-green/ excerpts from

the book that he and his team wrote in the 1980s, Spectral Suffolk.

5. Telephone interview with Phil Sage, 1 March 2014.

6. Cobbold, J. The Disappearing Garden. Amateur Gardening, 20 December 1975, pp.22-23.

7. Mackenzie, A. Adventures in Time, 1997.

8. Telephone interview with Sandra Newman (Hardwick), 5 May 2014.

9. Telephone interview with Phil Sage, 8 March 2014.

10. Telephone interview with Sandra Newman, 9 May 2014.

11. Wheatley, N. The Disappearing Garden. Suffolk Journal, June 1997, pp. 20-21.

12. Gooderham, D. "Ghostly mansion spotted in Suffolk." East Anglian Daily Times, 10 October

Time-Hopping: The Amazing Story of Ken Webster: Pages 126-135

Macy, Mark: Online, https://macyafterlife.com/2018/02/10/time-hopping-the-amazing-story-of-ken-webster/

The Rendlesham Forest Incident: Pages 136-142

[*49]He Touched A UFO! Sgt Penniston's Account!, page 1 /Forum
An excerpt from an interview with Sgt Jim Penniston concerning the Rendlesham Forest incident. Online www.abovetopsecret.com/forum/thread414407/pg1 accessed 12.11.2019. [*50]

wikipedia.org/wiki/Binary code][*51]

[*52] Hy Brasil, Hy Breasil, Hy Breasail, Hy Breasal, Hy Brazil, I-Brasil, Chisholm, Hugh, ed. (1911). "Brazil, or Brasil". Encyclopædia Britannica. 4 (11th ed.). Cambridge University Press. p. 438.

The Woolpit Case, Suffolk, England: Pages: 143-146

Cohen, Jeffrey Jerome (2008), "Green Children from Another World, or the Archipelago in England", in Cohen, Jeffrey Jeremy (ed.), Cultural Diversity in the British Middle Ages: Archipelago, Island, England, The New Middle Ages, Palgrave, pp. 75–94, ISBN 978-0-230-60326-4

Cosman, Pelner; Jones, Linda Gale (2008), Handbook to Life in the Medieval World, Facts On File, ISBN 978-0-8160-4887-8

Fanthorpe, Lionel; Fanthorpe, Patricia (2010), The Big Book of Mysteries, Dundurn Group, ISBN 978-1-55488-779-8

Harris, Paul (1998), "The Green Children of Woolpit: A 12th Century Mystery and its Possible Solution", in Moore, Steve (ed.), Fortean Studies: No. 4, John Brown Publishing, pp. 81–95, ISBN 978-1-870870-96-2

Haughton, Brian (2007), Hidden History: Lost Civilizations, Secret Knowledge, and Ancient Mysteries, New Page Books, ISBN 978-1-56414-897-1

Partner, Nancy F. (1977), Serious Entertainments: The Writings of History in Twelfth-Century England, University of Chicago Press, ISBN 978-0-226-64763-0

Citations

Clark, John (2006), "'Small, Vulnerable ETs': The Green Children of Woolpit", Science Fiction Studies, 33 (2): 209–229, JSTOR 4241432

Simpson, Jacqueline; Roud, Steve (2000), "Green Children", A Dictionary of English Folklore (online ed.), Oxford University Press, retrieved 5 April 2009

Lawton, H. W. (January 1931), "Bishop Godwin's Man in the Moone", The Review of English Studies, 7 (25): 23–55, doi:10.1093/res/os-vii.25.23, JSTOR 508383

Mills, A. D. (2003), "Woolpit", A Dictionary of British Place-Names, Oxford University Press, retrieved 25 April 2009 (subscription required)

Citations

Cosman & Jones 2008, p. 127

Briggs, K. M. (1970), "The Fairies and the Realms of the Dead", Folklore, 81 (2): 81–96, doi:10.1080/0015587X.1970.9716666, JSTOR 508383

Briggs 1967, p. 6

Clark, John (2006), "Martin and the Green Children", Folklore, 117 (2): 207–214, doi:10.1080/00155870600707904

Cohen 2008, p. 83

Lunan, Duncan (September 1996), "Children from the Sky", Analog Science Fiction and Science Fact, vol. 116 no. 11, pp. 38–53

Partner 1977, pp. 121–122

Orme, Nicholas (1995), "The Culture of Children in Medieval England", Past & Present, 148 (1): 48–88, doi:10.1093/past/148.1.48, JSTOR 651048

Oman, C. C. (1944), "The English Folklore of Gervase of Tilbury", Folklore, 55 (1): 2–15, doi:10.1080/0015587X.1944.9717702, JSTOR 1257623

Cohen 2008, p. 90

Baughman 1966, p. 203

Walsh, Martin W. (2000), "Medieval English Martinmesse: The Archaeology of a Forgotten Festival", Folklore, 111 (2): 231–254, doi:10.1080/00155870020004620, JSTOR 1260605

G. (24 February 1900), "Green Fairies: Woolpit Green Children", Notes and Queries, 5: 155

Haughton 2007, p. 236

Hutton, Sarah (Spring 2005), "The Man in the Moone and the New Astronomy: Godwin, Gilbert, Kepler" (PDF), Etudes Epistémè (7): 3–13... Harris 1998...

RECOMMENDED READING AND LINKS
Kevin Montana

www.messagetoeagle.com
Subjects we specialize in are cutting-edge science, astronomy, mind and brain, wonders of nature and unexplained phenomena.

Jenny Randles

Time Storms: The Amazing Evidence of Time Warps, Space Rifts and Time Travel
by Jenny Randles | 25 Jan 2001
TRULY WEIRD REAL LIFE CASES: Real-life Cases of the Paranormal
by Jenny Randles | 1 Oct 1998
Supernatural Pennines by Jenny Randles (2003-04-30) Paperback – 1998

Tom Slemen

Haunted Liverpool 31
by Tom Slemen | 31 Mar 2019
Haunted Liverpool 2
by Tom Slemen | 1 Nov 2014

Jim Penniston

The Rendlesham Enigma: Book 1: Timeline Paperback | 22 Jul 2019 by James W. Penniston (Author), Gary Osborn (Author)

Encounter in Rendlesham Forest: The Inside Story of the World's Best Documented UFO Incident: Nick Pope, with John Burroughs and Jim Penniston.

Theo Chalmers

Lloyd Pye: Where Did We Come From?
by Lloyd Pye, Theo Chalmers, et al.
Mysteries: Vampires, Oak Island, Time Machines, Psychics and More: by Lionel Fanthorpe Reverend, Theo Chalmers, et al.

C.R. Berry

Million Eyes by C.R. Berry
Million Eyes: Extra Time by C.R. Berry
Available on Amazon…

Ellie Crystal

Crystalinks is perhaps the largest, most comprehensive and ambitious metaphysical and science website on the Internet today.
https://www.crystalinks.com/

Scott Corrales

Chupacabras and Other Mysteries
Available on www.goodreads.com...
Website: http://inexplicata.blogspot.com

Andrew Collins

From the Ashes of Angels, Gods of Eden, Gateway to Atlantis, Tutankhamen. The Cygnus Mystery, Beneath the Pyramids, Göbekli Tepe: www.andrewcollins.com

Editor Bio: Graduate in Archaeology at the University of Manchester, formerly employed with the Civil Service in I.T support and administration. I also conduct archaeological research in rock carvings, and Prehistoric structures around the UK. My other interests include radio astronomy, creating websites and photography.

Printed in Great Britain
by Amazon